So That's How It Is

So That's How It Is

THE COMMONER

Copyright © 2018 by The Commoner.

ISBN:	Softcover	978-1-9845-2125-5
	eBook	978-1-9845-2124-8

All rights reserved. No part of this book may be reproduced or transmitted in any form or by any means, electronic or mechanical, including photocopying, recording, or by any information storage and retrieval system, without permission in writing from the copyright owner.

Any people depicted in stock imagery provided by Getty Images are models, and such images are being used for illustrative purposes only.
Certain stock imagery © Getty Images.

Print information available on the last page.

Rev. date: 04/10/2018

To order additional copies of this book, contact:
Xlibris
1-888-795-4274
www.Xlibris.com
Orders@Xlibris.com

CONTENTS

Chapter I: Who I am!..1

Chapter II: Moral turpitude -..17

Chapter III: The Roots of Governance -..................................21

Chapter IV: This Commoner's Thoughts about God! - 34

Chapter V: The Fall of a Nation - 50

Chapter VI: The Flip Side..85

Chapter VII: After thoughts - 90

Chapter VIII: Extrapolation of Consequences........................99

Chapter IX: Sunday Sermon!..111

Chapter X: Perspective on today's nation 120

Chapter XI: Tying It All Together - 140

CHAPTER I

Who I am!

I am a Commoner; generally perceived as "common labor" and the average consumer. Like all other Commoners, I exist at the bottom of the societal food chain that the rest of the world cannot do without, unless they want to do themselves in also. Social order mimics the natural order of nature. You have the predators at the top of the food chain that feed off lower members of the food chain, all the way down to the plankton and other microbial life forms. If you destroy the lower life forms then the next tier up starves to death because there's nothing left to feed off of and so the impact works its way up the food chain until the predator at the top suffers the same fate. There is a category of humanity that has ALWAYS exploited the Commoner as a means of achieving wealth, power and authority while we commoners are most comfortable staying out of that fray and just want to take life slow and easy. Unfortunately, such an attitude is what makes us the prey and makes us prime targets for manipulation and exploitation, which is what this is all about. One of the hallmarks of freedom, that we no longer enjoy, was the freedom to be a loaner and live isolated lives away from civilization, more specifically, government. Many of our pioneers pursued this kind of life and we have a few today that have managed to find a place of isolation for themselves. For the rest of us, we are forced by circumstance to be a part of the group order called society and civilization. We have become so populated that there is no more free space where government isn't up your backside. Even those that have found a remote spot in the wilderness end up having to interact with some government, at some level, at some point in time.

I was born in upper state New York but was raised in the High Plains of Kansas and the hills of the Ozarks. In 1944, when I was born, we considered ourselves to be a very developed nation, way ahead of all the other countries. In fact, we were kind of smug about it and had no problem making fun of those of lesser development who thought they could conquer us. Little did we know that we would become our own worst enemy as we began to take things for granted and our culture began to morph into something considerably less desirable. (Spoiled brats become spoiled brats because they get catered too all of their lives and don't have to pay the price like everybody else. Everything becomes valueless until they get knocked down and no longer have their toys or privileges.)

I was born with ADD, (self diagnosed), and so book learning was not exactly my forte. I looked at the world as a world to be explored and experienced and being born into poverty doesn't exactly lend itself to such desires. I wanted to experience and test the waters of everything I came into contact with or heard about or saw on TV, (which was in its infancy back then). I wanted to know, and still do, what makes everything tick. Unfortunately, for my adventurous spirit, there were a lot of disciplines out there that require a lot of book learning and a head for mathematics and formulas, etc., and I recognize my limitations. That still didn't prevent me from experiencing as much as I could about them. I obviously couldn't become a doctor but I did spend a few years working for the engineering department of a prominent hospital. I suck at the fine points of navigation and swim like a rock but I spent a bunch of years with the Navy as a Seabee and got to taste the life of a sailor and experience their many disciplines; (I still suck at navigation and still swim like a rock)! I spent time in the Air Force, (stuck behind a desk), but I got to work in the control tower and participate in the experience of being an airman. Things didn't pan out all that well for me but I still got an honorable for my short tour of duty. My regret is that I didn't just transfer to one of the other branches of service, instead of opting out, and making a career of it. I've been forced into leadership positions by attrition or because a job needed to be done and nobody else would step up to the plate, (which I would have preferred). I envied the life of the lumberjack; tried it, wasn't physically fit enough to follow through with that. Have a lot of respect for those guys! According to the stats, it's the most dangerous profession in the world, leading all professions in fatality rates and injuries. Twenty two times more dangerous than being a cop! (At least back then it was. We have a corrupt society today, punks raised by our generations and our previous generations, that have put targets on their, (the cop's), backs for doing their job. And then they are miffed as to why some are trigger happy!)

My father, grandfather and great grandfather were all carpenters. During their era, there was no specialization of trades, so to speak. If you were a carpenter/contractor, you had to know it all and be able to do it all; at least if you lived outside the populated areas and the city slickers. Kansas is farm and cattle country and so a lot of our carpentry experience was associated with farms and ranches and the residential construction of small country towns. Learning how to do carpentry was inevitable but not binding.

My mother was one of the Harvey Girls, (at least that is what she told me), and apparently she met my father through a USO event where she was volunteering. Being a Harvey Girl back then was like being one of Hugh Heffner's Playboy Bunnies and a pin up girl for the soldiers. She was a beautiful woman back then but then something snapped in her head and things went downhill very quickly from then on. She split from my father, taking us kids with her and then she abandoned my brother and sister and took me back to New York with her to start a new life. We moved in with her mother, whom I loved and adored, but my mother's attitude couldn't be tolerated and we overstayed our welcome. She went to her estranged father for help and after a bunch of bellering, she got permission to use one of his hunting cabins out by a place called Millt's Corner. There was a filling station on the corner there, just walking distance from the little one-room cabin. I used to go there and buy Kayo Chocolate Drink for a nickel and a Powerhouse, (I think it was called that), candy bar for 3-cents. I would gather up empty soda bottles from along the side of the highway and cash them in for two or three cents on the bottle. Coke bottles would get me a nickel.

The cabin had a propane cook stove, (but no propane), and a couple of lights but that was it. Winter was coming on and the cabin had no heat or insulation. It was drafty! We woke up one morning and the floor of most all the cabin was covered with a layer of ice. We bundled up as best we could and would wrap ourselves in the blankets to help keep us warm. We spent Christmas there! Mom cleaned houses for people and a couple of them helped mom with some Christmas presents for me. A church was throwing out an old upright piano which she got to bring home and I got a geography game that allowed you to connect the capitals to their states with a jumper wire which would cause a little buzzer and light to come on when you got it right. I got the "Operation" game that would light up the patient's nose if you grounded out the slot that the part you were removing was in. The other thing I got was a small, plastic train that you get from the gumball machines. That was our Christmas! I think mom brought home some leftovers from somebody else's dinner for our Christmas dinner.

By spring, mom had enough money together to get an apartment in a small town nearby, down by the river front. It was an upstairs apartment with another old propane stove. I remember it well because I thought I would make mom some molasses cookies while she was away at work. I poured little puddles of molasses here and there on a cookie sheet and popped it in the oven. Fortunately for the apartment, she came home in time to catch the error of my ways and prevented me from burning down the house.

The neighborhood wasn't one of the friendliest of neighborhoods. I would get into a fight nearly every time I stepped out the front door and onto the porch. My birthday came up in May and mom bought me a chemistry set for my birthday. I read through the booklet that came with it and then I took my chemistry set to the stoop on the front porch. It wasn't long before my antagonists came along but then instead of instigating fights, they wanted to see what I could do with the chemistry set. Unlike today's kiddie chem-sets, I was able to make certain petty explosives, kind of firecracker size, from the set and all of a sudden I had a lot of friends. It wasn't too long after that, that I guess the manufacturer modified the chemistry set to eliminate the pyrotechnics; disappointing!

I used to go across the street to the water's edge and watch the fishermen fish from shore. About the only thing they caught was Carp but they were huge. They were every bit as big as I was and that really impressed me. It was after this that my mother had a nervous breakdown and had to be institutionalized and so her mother took me in but it was only for a short time. Grandma was diagnosed with spinal cancer and told that she didn't have much time left to live and that her pain would get progressively worse and that there was nothing they could do for her. I was made a ward of the state and sent to a foster home that was out in the country. Mom was unresponsive, grandma laid up and nobody knew where my father was. I was in the foster home for about a year before the state located my father and it was able to arrange my return to him. (I think I was in the 2nd grade around then. Grandma suffered with her cancer for years after that and died while I was in the Air Force. They wouldn't allow me to attend her funeral and that caused some resentment which influenced my desire to leave the Air Force.)

The foster home was a dairy farm and milk was gathered by machine and by hand. I wasn't much more than a toddler at the time; I think I might have been in either the 1st grade or 2nd. It was the Buttercup Dairy Farm and there was Mrs. Buttercup, (never got to know her first name), Max Buttercup and Pete Buttercup. I called them Uncle Max and Uncle Pete. Uncle Pete took me under his wing which offered me some respite from the rest of the family which wasn't too keen on me. They had a daughter named Marg, (if memory serves me right), who couldn't have been more spoiled. Lunch boxes were made of heavy metal back then and she would use hers as a weapon of choice against me and everybody else on the school bus. Of course, Grandma Buttercup did nothing about it. None of us were allowed in the house except at meal time and to go to bed and that made for a miserable winter. Pete would take me fishing and allow me to ride on the tractor with him. He put me to work in the dairy barn shoveling manure and learning how to milk cows. I got myself gored by one of the Jersey Cows; nothing serious but I learned where not to be. I helped gather eggs and then he taught me how to candle them and pack them for shipment. They raised Arkansas Red Razor Back hogs and I would help slop them. I was never allowed in that area without him present because they were somewhat vicious and had large tusks that could tear you apart. I had specific instructions to climb a nearby tree if they got aggressive while we were in there. To me, they were about the size of a small horse and ten times heavier.

I can't remember for sure what time of the year it was, other than it was still warm weather, but we had been out in one of the fields doing some disking when he had me walk back to the farm to get some water for us to drink. I was about half way there when one of the hands drove down the access road and told me that the farm was on fire and that I needed to get hold of Uncle Pete. Obviously, that wasn't going to happen because he drove off and left me standing there as he went to inform Uncle Pete himself. They shot right past me on the way back there and left me to walk the distance back to the farm house, about ¾ of a mile. The fire was intense and we lost nearly everything. The barn was a three story barn with the bottom reserved for a milk shed, pig pen for baby pigs, (I think it's called a farrowing pen), and machine storage. The first loft was hay and the third loft was straw, all very incendiary and both lofts very full! At the front entrance to the barn was a loading dock for milk pick ups and a silo full of silage saturated with alcohol from natural fermentation. The farmstead had a horseshoe drive with a pump house/garage in the middle of it and at the top of the horseshoe, at the back of the lot, was the chicken house and woodshed. On the other side of the horseshoe drive was the house and its outhouse.

Apparently one of the hands had set an open gas can in the pump shed and the heat of the day caused the can to fill the shed with gasoline fumes. When the water pump kicked on, the sparks ignited the fumes which resulted in a huge explosion. The hand, (can't remember his name), that put the can in the shed was sitting in the outhouse at the time and, from what I was told, blew him and its door out onto the pathway. It broke some of the windows in the farm house and I guess most of the blast exited the pump room door towards the silo which instantly caught fire and then everything literally exploded with fire from that point on. There were no cows in the barn so we didn't lose any of them but the piglets lost their lives; nobody could get to them because of the heat. The fire was so hot that it burned one of the responding firetrucks where it was parked out on the road a good 50-yards from the barn, I think, and seared the side of the house in spite of firefighters keeping it hosed down. We lost the chicken house and woodshed and all the farm equipment that was in storage at the time. The day before, myself and their farmhand had caught a huge snapping turtle and we had put it in an old freezer that we used for keeping milk in until pick up time, (it was empty and turned off). The turtle was smoke and the ice chest was nothing more than a blob of metal laying in the ruins. All metals in there were melted, including the milking machines, (they only had two, the rest of the milking was done by hand).

I don't remember much about what went on after that fire. I think I remember some of the cement blocks were being laid for the new barn but I'm not for sure. It was around this time that the state had found my father and had arranged for me to be returned home. I would be flying home by myself and at a time when the air industry was still in its early days. The first plane was a three wheeler plane like was seen in the movie Casablanca. It had a pair of wheels under the wings and a little wheel under the tail end and you got on by using a little step stool like thingy that they rolled up to the door. The second plane they put me on was a turboprop plane which took me from Chicago to Kansas City and the third was a similar style plane with four props. On the plane from Chicago to Kansas City, a young man next to me was asked to watch over me while the hostesses did their thing and he agreed, no problem! I found out later in the flight that he was a cowboy movie star; I still didn't have a clue, never heard of him before. It wasn't until I got home and settled in that I got to watch TV with the rest of the kids and there he was, in the saddle and riding the range.

My father had remarried while I was away and had married the Wicked Witch of the West, as far as I was concerned. She was a petite, Irish red head with a fiery temper and a bad attitude. She was just plane mean! She put us kids to work helping her to do the cooking, cleaning, laundry, gardening and you name it and if we weren't sprite enough or efficient enough to suit her, she would take a willow switch to us and literally cut us to ribbons with it. She had a son, (would be one of my younger step brothers), who had mental issues and was a kleptomaniac. You couldn't walk anywhere near him without losing something to his slight-of-hand. One day he stole a dollar bill from her and put it in my glass coin jar in place of the coins he stole from it. When she figured things out, she took him into the kitchen and held his hands in the fire on the stove until they blistered to teach him not to steal. It didn't cure him! He did it again and she did it again. Not Kosher! The coins he took were from my coin collection, which included one of America's first coins. I think it was a penny but it was the size of a silver dollar. (I found it wedged under the edge of an old bench in the train station where I arrived in New York with my mother.) I had Indian Heads, Standing Liberties and a couple of three legged buffalo nickels. He spent them around town and when the word got out about what he had done, we had a boost in the economy as coin collectors swooped in to buy out the coins in all the vending machines in town in search of my coins. A couple of the kids set the house on fire twice while I was away in the service by playing with matches in the upstairs closet. In addition to the coins, I also had a rock collection, which included agates, Amethysts and a few other semi-precious stones and a stamp collection with some of America's earlier stamps and stamps from around the world. Lost all of that when they burned the house down!

This was a small farming community. At first we were renting a house in the country on a piece of farm land owned by another dairy farmer. We would buy our milk from him and I loved it. It provided us with home churned butter and cheese and fresh cream to pour over a bowl full of fresh picked strawberries. It didn't have running water but it did have electric and an old crank phone/party line where you'd give a couple of cranks on the the phone and it would ring the operator who would answer and ask you who you wanted to talk to. She would then use a jumper from your line and plug it into the other person's line and then give a series of rings that told them that it was for them and you would be connected. What's significant about this is that I would eventually become a member of the construction crew that traveled throughout the area replacing that old system with buried cable and new dial-up phones that allowed you to dial direct to the person you wanted to talk to; the "party line" was now history!

I don't know how dad did it, but he managed to get the financing to buy up three pieces of property there. The old two story was the one we moved into and made our final home. The other two were flip properties which he sold to pay off the mortgages and finish paying for the house and nearly half of the city block that it was on. One of the city officials told us that the one house we flipped used to belong to Dwight Eisenhower's parents when they were young. Imagine that!

My stepmother turned all that acreage into a vegetable farm with a pig pen and a hen house. This is where I learned how to cook, can, butcher and preserve! I didn't have to join FFA or FHA; I was getting the lessons in real time, first hand at home and it wasn't a hobby or an adventure. Learning wasn't optional! My older stepbrothers were into mechanics and race cars and so I learned how to work on cars from them. Two of my favorite cars was the Edsel and the Henry J. Probably because they were totally different from any other car on the market! Personally, I thought they were classier looking than the other cars of the day. At least they were different! It was here that I learned to drive. By the time I was ten, I was driving a grain truck. My job was to keep it in position under the auger of the combine as it moved through the field and dumped its harvest into the bed of the truck. Of course, an adult would take it to the co-op for storage or processing! I was so small that I had to stand to see over the hood of the truck and still reach the pedals. The first car I drove was an old Hudson Clipper. I presume it was a Clipper because it had medallions on the inside of the doors that had the picture of a clipper ship on them. All transportation back then was manual shift. Automatics weren't around yet.

In the summer time, the folks would take us to live with my stepmother's mother, deep in the Ozarks, a little ways from a small town up in the Northwest corner of the state, deep in the mountains of Arkansas. She lived in an old log cabin that was completely off the grid; no amenities whatsoever. We hauled water from a creek at the bottom of the mountain and fetched drinking water from a spring hidden deep in the woods on the side of the mountain. According to my oldest stepbrother, the spring used to be the entrance to one of America's only diamond mines but the Corp of Engineers dynamited it shut as it was considered just too dangerous for anybody to be in. It was full of thousands of rattle snakes and very unstable. Quite the deadly combination! At least that is what I was told! I recently heard that there is another diamond mine near Little Rock but I haven't done too much research into that. It does make me wish I had the money to buy the old cabin site and land to go prospecting and go off-grid like she did. My time there on that mountain top is one of my favorite memories. I had a couple of cousins that were Native American Indians who lived on a reservation with their parents. They came to visit there for a short while and they shared with me some of the hunting lessons that they had learned from their elders. One of the tests for being a hunter was how well you could stalk your prey. They taught me how to stalk and catch wildlife with my bare hands. We had a lot of fun doing that. We caught quail and pheasant with our bare hands; I'm not sure I could do that today. Let's just say I'm pleasingly plump today and was a wisp of a human being back then.

The cabin had a loft that overlooked the main room downstairs. The kitchen was a lean-to that was built onto the back of the cabin after the fact and was equipped with a wood stove. Just about everything eaten there was home grown. Paul, one of my older stepbrothers, owned an old, beat up pick up and he would use that to go into town and get essentials like flour and salt or even a bag of cookies. He also used it to haul water from the creek for granny to do laundry with. She had a huge cast iron cauldron out in the front yard that she would build a fire under to heat up the wash water. She would get out the scrub board and do the laundry pioneer style and with home made lye soap. One of the better stories I took from there was when she took an iron skillet out the front door of the cabin and over to the fence line to dump out its grease. She felt the dog running its nose up the backside of her dress and turned and cold-cocked it with the skillet. It wasn't the dog! It was a small black bear. She said her feet didn't touch the ground she was moving so fast to get in the cabin before it came too.

When we hauled the water, some of us had to sit in the back of the truck and steady the 55-gal drums of water as we made our way back up the mountain. On one trip, Chip lost his balance and flipped out of the bed of the truck and landed in a bed of cactus. He was picking needles out of himself for days after that. On another occasion, Paul took me with him to go get some groceries. On the way back we had opened a package of cookies and was munching away when he lost control of the truck and we went up one side of a hill, through the trees and back down the other side and back onto the road before we got stopped. He ended up in my place in the passenger seat and I was hanging out his driver side window. We kept that incident from everybody for years. I'm not sure granny ever found out.

The cabin had a home made bed frame with a home-made feather mattress set next to the door to the front of the room where Paul slept and we used an old bench style car seat for a couch which set in the middle of the room in front of a huge fire place that had a swing-arm assembly with a cauldron hanging from that. It could swing in and out over the fire in the fireplace to regulate the cooking heat of the cauldron. Behind the car seat was the dining table where we all sat. There were two beds in the loft that were home made feather beds, king size. A half dozen of us would arrange ourselves on each bed to sleep. The walls were wallpapered with copies of old newspapers. One catching my attention, carried an article about a new invention, automatic transmissions, and was airing a debate about whether they would be sturdy enough and efficient enough for use in trucks and semi's. Can you imagine reading about a debate over whether an automatic could compete with a manual transmission? That's history up front and personal! The cabin was forever covered with mud-masons, (a small black wasp that made its nest out of mud) and we'd have to argue with them over sleeping rights almost every evening. This is where I learned from grandma about how to treat bee stings. It was really simple! Just lather on some rich, loam mud and let it sit. It took out the pain and suffering and facilitated healing immensely. Of course, you wanted to remove the stinger first, if the bee managed to leave one behind. She also taught us about wild herbs, flowers and roots which had certain medicinal qualities and she didn't just share them with us. She had contracts with a couple of pharmaceutical companies to provide them to them, (pre-processed), and to teach them how to use them. Between learning her pioneer skills and how to live off the land from my parents, I developed some very good survival skills, but very few social skills. I'm not necessarily people friendly. I prefer to keep to myself and commune with nature. Don't like crowds and don't like the hustle, bustle of city life. For me, city life sucks! It's like being free to roam around the confines of a huge prison and that's your world! Your entire perspective on life is based on life inside your prison and on your interactions with other prisoners that can't comprehend what freedom is.

Anyhow, I got tired of being one of my mother's whipping posts and decided to run away from home when I was 16. I managed to stay away for almost a year before I got caught and brought back. As soon as I got brought back, I walked eight miles to a nearby town where I signed up to join the Air Force. Unfortunately, I wasn't old enough to be inducted but my birthday was only a couple weeks away and then, with my father's written permission, I could enlist in the Air Force, which I did! Color me gone! Me and the Air Force didn't get along too well. They liked neatly pressed uniforms, shiny shoes and polished brass; I liked dirt, mud and oil! They wanted me in an office and I wanted to wallow in the swamp! They gave me an acuity test, don't know what they really called it; but it was to assess where my skills lay. I pretty much scored the same in all categories. I guess you could call that a typical "Red Neck" score! I chose the Air Force because I wanted to fly. Unfortunately I was grunt material, not officer material with college credits, and so I chose to be a weather man. Alas, I became an apprentice Weather Observer! Their training was lacking and not nearly as good as it is today. I remained in the Air Force for one year, three months and thirteen days and was honorably discharged. If had known then what I know now, I would have simply transferred over to the Navy where I would have fit in beautifully with the Seabees. About a decade later I joined the Active Naval Reserve as a Seabee. I loved it in spite of not getting the billet that I wanted. They took me in as a mechanic because of my mechanic skills but what they needed was a company clerk that understood the paper work and the UCMJ and guess what, I was back behind a desk shuffling papers! At least this time I got to get out of the office from time to time and travel with my mates and actually worked within my billet as a mechanic. I also got to train with the Marines and Special Forces and the Army, (cross-training to familiarize us with their systems and programs so that we could provide flawless support). The people in my unit were among some of the best people I've ever known. I was with them for around 14-years, honorable discharge.

After that, I attended a college in Colorado until I ran out of money and employment; I had to hitch rides back to Kansas in the dead of winter with nothing more than the clothes on my back. Fortunately, I did very little walking and a lot of riding and worked my way back to a small border town in western Kansas where I earned my keep repairing washers and dryers in a laundromat. While there, I made a friend that introduced me to welding and taught me how to be a first class ironworker. During the winter layoffs, we went to work in a factory where I made another friend who ditched a date for a gig with a band. I hooked up with his date and married her. When they closed the factory where I worked, I went to work on a cattle ranch, (25,000 acres and 500 head prime Black Angus). Again, I was living pretty much off grid. We had electric lights but that was about it. The house was nearing the 100 year mark and one of the cowboys that worked with me helped haul the lumber used to build the house and actually had an encounter with Indians once while doing so. At least that was his story! I'm certain the house was at least a hundred years old which means that he couldn't have possibly hauled the lumber for its construction. (He was in his late eighties and still cowboying!) He showed me where the old Sante Fe Trail cut through our pastures and where the corner posts of his cabin were with only the tops sticking out of the soil after it got buried during a dust storm. He still carried a wild west revolver when we herded cattle from the bottoms to the high grounds and he was a crack shot with it. We would invite him in whenever we could just to listen to his adventures from almost 80 years prior, (the late 1800's). Again, history up front and personal!

When I got word that my father was dying, I deemed it necessary to pack up and leave the ranch and head home to take care of his affairs. Somebody in the family screwed me over! There wasn't anything wrong with him but by the time I got there and found that out, the owner of the ranch had already sold the ranch to a mega-farmer that was already farming at least a million acres of land. He seemed to be about as cold-hearted as a person could be. He just started bulldozing everything and completely isolated the lands from anybody and everybody. I haven't been back since.

After working around the home area for awhile, (which included installing the new phone system), we hooked up with an Evangelistic Association where we worked as roustabouts, assistant evangelists and as missionaries at home and in Mexico. He enrolled me in a seminary's correspondence course. After a near-death experience from tainted salsa, we came back to the United States where I found work as an ironworker for awhile, (worked myself out of a job), and then got an invite to move to Florida, "where the jobs are!" Wasn't a good move! I found work with a condo association, running their maintenance operations, and then went to work for one of the area's largest hospitals in their engineering and maintenance department. My son was born while I was working for the condo association and then I went to work for the hospital. My wife was pregnant with a girl and took sick around the first part of December. I presented her with her Christmas presents while she was confined to the hospital bed and in February my daughter was still born and the following week, the love of my life passed as well. I have forever regretted not having hugged her enough and not having told her how much I loved her. You never realize how much you love somebody until the day comes that you can no longer hold them, kiss them goodnight or share your day with them.

In the mean time, I was saddled with a one year old baby that needed constant attention. I needed affordable child care so that I could earn a living. The problem with child care is that its cost cuts your usable income by about half. A friend of one of her friends offered to babysit for me but the caveat to that was catching him when he wasn't drunk. There were many occasions when I had to take him to work with me where understanding and caring nurses would help keep an eye on him while I answered calls. A couple years later, while searching the bar scene for my babysitter, I came across another woman in dire straits. She saw me leave the tavern and came running after me to get protection from a stalker, (in the bar), that had threatened to cut her if she took off. When he went into the restroom, she made a break for it; straight to me. I had her duck down in the back seat of the car so that her pursuer couldn't see her and I went back and met him at the door. He wanted to know which way she went and I sent him off on a wild goose chase. Piece of cake! She was divorced and had two girls in her custody and a son that was in his father's custody. About a half year later, we got married. She was a nice woman but she had issues and so did her kids. It was unfortunate for my son that he got caught in the middle of all this, which was detrimental to his upbringing. All kinds of bad things happened that escaped my knowledge until after she passed away, (in the month of February, same day as my daughter).

She had a gambling habit! For the longest time, I couldn't figure out why we kept getting evicted from our homes. She'd tell me it was because the landlord was going to fix up the property and give it to their son or they sold the property or they were going to gut the place and remodel. Seemed like a lot of bad vibes to me. After she passed, the kids clued me in. She was taking the rent money I gave her and spending it on Bingo. She would always come home thrilled because she hit the $100 jackpot but it didn't compute in her head that she spent the rent getting there. She developed kidney disease and after about 15 years of marriage, she passed away from kidney failure and other complications.

A couple of years after she passed, I started dating a new friend but I was very hesitant about taking things any farther than the dating. We had an expressed love for each other but we didn't have the chemistry for a relationship beyond that. We could only be cooped up together for a few hours and we'd begin to get on each other's nerves. I had two marriages where things went fairly well and I didn't want to have a marriage where things could get contentious and end with us not liking each other. She was diabetic and developed three different types of cancers to which she succumbed about a year or so later. Strike three! I haven't had any social life since!

My last occupation was for a municipality. I was a heavy equipment operator/driver for the municipality, (Solid Waste Division/garbage man), and stayed with them for 22 years until I retired. I joined the union while there and held every office in the local, including president. It was the union that got me active in politics and community service. I was president of the local, founding president of our neighborhood association & crime watch and had a delivery business on the side. Burning the candle at all ends, just trying to make ends meet! This is where my activism began and where I got educated on party politics, lobbying and political tactics.

I was president of the local when a salesman came around with this little thing that looked like a TV. He was selling personal computers and I got to looking it over and decided that we could use one of those things to do a lot of the local's paper work. It was a real pain at first because it didn't have enough memory capacity to run the programs you needed to process the information, let alone write a letter or produce the membership roles. We upgraded when upgrades were possible and I finagled my way around to getting a PC of my own, with a printer. I enjoyed using it immensely and then the world introduced the internet and now I am an information addict. I'm computer illiterate because I couldn't keep up with technology but I love surfing the internet! I can research any topic and cross reference everything I come across so as to vet it. It's like having the Library of Congress at your finger tips! Fantastic! Now I have a broad perspective of the world around me and everything that's going on. Now I just have to figure out when to sleep!

CHAPTER II

Moral turpitude -

I consider myself a Christian but on the other hand, I'm not a very religious person. I believe in the KJ New Testament and Christ but I don't worship the Bible as though it is some kind of God like the extremists do and take things to the extreme. I take into consideration that its words, inspired of God or not, is the product of humans, a flawed creature to say the least! Most of the places spoken of in the Old Testament and thought to have been mythology, have been found, thereby vetting most of the scriptures. I look at the Bible as a bibliography of humanity. It is a record of humanity's quest for righteousness among themselves. We can read about humanity's trial and error methodology for determining what their morals, ethics, values and virtues would have been under their circumstances and why; I believe that my perception of that process is undebatable! When we read those scriptures we should be looking at the lessons learned and how they came to their conclusions, whether it is the Book of Moses (Genesis), or the Psalms or the Book of Proverbs. They are all lessons in humanity's character and behavior over the centuries and it would benefit us to pay attention to them and embrace the lessons learned. As for their veracity, I take into account that the people that translated the ancient texts and decided what would go into our copy of the Bible and what would not, (like the Book of Enoch or the Chronicles of Lilith), are the same people that murdered people by crucifixion and torture for believing that the earth was round and not the center of the universe and orchestrated the Spanish Inquisitions. That's not very good credentials for putting all your eggs in their basket!

Extremism drives people away from you, not invite you in! One needs to keep in mind too, that the people of all the other religions believe that their beliefs are the truth just as much as we believe that ours is the truth. I believe that we have the truth but the evidence supporting our faith is no more validatable than the evidence that the other faiths believe they have. We used to have the Ark of the Covenant and the Ten Commandments written on stone slabs and brought down from the mountain by Moses but those have long since gone into oblivion.

On top of all of this, there is another consideration that is getting serious attention. There is the theory that what we took to be gods, angels or demons were really extraterrestrials and that we were the result of a genesis project or some other kind of experiment. Many of the pictographs and hieroglyphics found on the stones of ancient sites, art work and writings conform very much to current beliefs about aliens and parallels in technology, like batteries, lights, flight and archaeological evidence of advanced surgery techniques and construction techniques that we can't mimic with today's technologies lead to that hypothesis. Denying and ignoring this stuff isn't going to make it go away or invalidate it. It doesn't invalidate my perception of God or the Gospel either, though, because my God is a God of the entire universe, not just earth and our scriptures were written by earthlings for earthlings and have nothing to do with the rest of the universe. We haven't a clue about what God was doing beyond the earth nor do we have a clue about how He might have brought things to bear upon the earth, such as using beings from other worlds. If one of them showed up today, we'd probably think they were somebody with super natural powers because of how much more advanced they would be over us in knowledge, skills, technology and understandings. There's a lot of room for speculation and we cannot be hanging on to superstition and superstitious beliefs over validated evidence to our own detriment. I haven't seen anything to dissuade me from my beliefs but I have had to accept the fact that some of that which was mystical and which was described in a religious sense was technology that we take for granted today. There are significant events in the Bible that cannot be debunked and others are validated and that lends to its credibility in spite of archaeological conflicts. I'm staying the course!

I like to play Solitary and I like to play it with a strategic methodology, like one would play a game of chess. Many times I'll sit and stare at the cards for as much as a half hour and not see the moves available to me until I walk away and come back later. (Solitaire is more than just putting colored cards on opposing cards. It's knowing when to play them so as to facilitate multiple moves and not block future moves.) When I come back, like magic, I see the plays and am completely miffed over why I couldn't see them earlier.

The Bible is the same way! We can read it and read it and it won't make sense to us and yet a year later we'll read over the same passages and a light bulb goes off in our heads and we perceive what we couldn't figure out before. The scriptures themselves tell you that most of them are intended to be cryptic to the non believer and will remain so until you become a believer and then as you grow in the spirit, more and more of the mystery scriptures are revealed to you for your understanding. Take it for what it's worth! In spite of the possibility of flaws caused by flawed human beings doing the writing, I stand by the Bible and the New Testament and do believe that it was inspired of God. Man just happens to be God's version of Murphy's Law; if there's a way to screw things up, count on us! Follow Christ's advice, "in all things, do so in MODERATION"! In other words, don't be taking things to the extreme.

Today, I'm retired and spend much of my time analyzing our society's history and the evolving evolution of our culture/s and government and I've found that we are embroiled in a negative algorithm that threatens our existence as a nation and is more of a threat to our existence than any enemy anywhere in the world. Our country is in social decay on multiple levels as evidenced by the decline in moral turpitude, ethics and virtues that used to provide stability to our civilization. We have natural born enemies among us that have no use for the restrictions that morals, religion and the Constitution impose on them. They want free reign to impose their beliefs or take advantage of everybody else and sincerely believe that they are of superior intellect and thereby should rule over everybody else whether they like it or not! They have no problem lying, cheating, stealing or even facilitating murders to achieve their goals. To quote one of them, "The end justifies the means!" That quote gives them license to flush their morals, honor and image down the sewer to achieve their agenda and feel justified in doing it. That way their act doesn't prick their conscience and make them feel guilty of having done wrong.

These factors and the lessons learned from history is the framework by which I evaluate what is going on in our society and what direction our behavior and character is taking us. We are not headed in the right direction!

CHAPTER III

The Roots of Governance -

The family structure is the template for governance; it is a natural design of nature, a monarchy! Obviously, there had to have been the first couple, (Adam & Eve?), and generation after generation of descendants with the parents of each generation succeeding Adam & Eve's first generation of offspring, being the rulers over their own offspring, Adam and Eve's grand-kids, etc. After Cain and Able, they produced 86 more offspring. That in itself is a tribe and would require some organizing in order to take care of the family and the delegating of responsibilities and tasks. If all their offspring were as productive as mom and pop then each generation is going to expand exponentially to the 86th power, into a community and then a nation in very short order. Each set of parents is part of the monarchical blood line with the eldest taking over as the head of the family when the parents die. I think it's pretty safe to say that our first form of government was a monarchy.

    Its obvious that dictators have their roots in greed and take what they want by force and use force to impose their brand of governance, such as what happened in Cuba when Castro overthrew Jean-Bertrand Aristide. Aristide was a vicious despot and Fidel recruited support by telling them that he would bring democracy to Cuba and bring an end to the corruption. They ended up trading one pole-cat for another! Castro never kept his word.

Democracy is attributed to the Greeks. I don't know what caused them to change the game, perhaps taking a vote on what to have for dinner and then deciding to apply that to government! In the end even that process got corrupted by the political agendas of their detractors. "Et tu Brutè!"

Our form of government was the first of its kind, chosen by the people and founded under the principle that all men are created equal and therefore nobody has a right to dominate over others without their consent. Alas, "government by the consent of the governed", a first! We are a representative form of government which has canonized human rights into its Constitution and established limitations on the different levels of government, delegating the final authority to the people. Thus, a government "of the People, By the People and For the People." We set the standard for what a government should be and a number of countries around the world chose to emulate our type of government within their own structures. That is something to be proud of!

During the first century and a half or so, we prospered and grew like we were on steroids but then it seems we peaked out and began to lose our edge. After having gone through the Great Depression and WWII, we began to regain momentum and then all of a sudden we peaked out and began to decline industrial wise, socially, economically and culturally. It seemed like bad news was coming from all directions. Economically, we went from a family being able to comfortably survive off of one income to needing multiple incomes per household for the "Commoner", (which represents over half the population). The socioeconomic distribution of the population reflects the pyramid structure of the typical business or industrial setup. You've got the one percenters and three percenters at the top; the managers, department heads, etc., in the middle and all the worker bees at the bottom of the pyramid within similar percentage parameters.

If you want to figure out what one of the things wrong with our economic system is then start listening to the political debates, news broadcasts and the advertising. The whole nine yards is focused on the economics of the middle class, including the pricings in the marketplace. (There's two "market places. One is Wall Street and the other is where we go shopping!) With marketplace items priced to accommodate the Middle Class's finances, it leaves the Commoner scratching for the table scraps. A business isn't primarily executives and owners; it is full of commoners, common labor. They are the people that do the hands on of production. They also represent the majority of recurring market demand as they purchase what they need for their day to day survival needs.

There are three tiers to our economic structure and the success of the top two tiers are dependent on the success of the bottom tier. Our problem is that Corporate America and its politicians refuse to acknowledge this financial algorithm. The top two tiers have control over ¾ of the liquid assets of this country. (The fractions and percentages cited are for emphasis on disparity and not a precise representation of the disparity.) The majority of the population, the commoners, are relegated to dividing up the remaining 25% between us on a per capita basis. Of course the distribution isn't going to be equal because everybody is of a different value to different employers who are subject to market demand pricing on the end product. We commoners are the primary source for cash flow within the economy at our level. Market demand is dependent upon our ability to facilitate cash flow between the time clock and the cash register. The more cash flow we can facilitate, the healthier the economy and the more vibrant both marketplaces become.

The Middle Class involves wages, salaries and investment returns. Some demand high incomes working on the clock while others get paid a straight salary without time restrictions on hours worked and, because of their much better salaries, tend to have investment portfolios and retirement plans that are structured around investment portfolios. That is a much different economic tier than that of the commoner. Fewer people means less influence on the market, the commoner's market. A business might have a thousand employees spending maybe twenty dollars a day each on grub but it'll only have maybe 25 mid-level employees, (department heads and executives, etc.), that will be spending about the same amount each. That common labor is going to spend about $25,000 a day for its eats while the 25 mid-level employees are going to spend maybe $625 a day for that same grub. Big difference in the economic impact. I don't care how rich the owner is, he's still only going to need $25 worth of food, hardly enough to sustain the cash flow of the economy. As I have shown here, the majority of the population, which are the working class/common labor, is the majority shareholder of market demand.

This is critical information because this relationship is ignored by business and industry and their politicians. Corporate America controls the time clock which determines what the majority of the influx of cash into the economy is going to be. They also control the cash register which defines the cost of living. In short, they control the influx and efflux of cash within the economy. They don't get it! We are the facilitators of that cash flow as we take what we earn and exchange it at the cash register for what we need for our survival. That is the economy in a nut shell. All else is incidental to that algorithm. If we can't compete with the cost of living, as established by business and industry at the cash register, then market demand is suppressed. Without market demand business and industry loses the impetus to stay in business and so they have to cut back production and lay people off which compounds the suppression of the market and the degeneration of our economy on all levels as their actions suppress cash flow. (Our marketplace is where we go shopping. Wall Street is its own marketplace and is dependent upon the economic wellness of the Middle Class and Elite who wheel and deal in the stock market. Their world is not our world!) When you hear the media talking about how great the market is doing, they are not talking about our market; they're talking about the Middle Class's market – Wall Street!

Now, for the Elite/Upper Class! This is where the grass root population is being played by the politicians. Everybody wants to jump on the bandwagon to stick it to the elite and demand super high income taxes. News Flash: read your 1040's for what constitutes "income". Time clock pay and salaries are income that is affected by "income taxes!" Other income sources are not subject to the income tax. In other words, it doesn't matter what you jack the income taxes to, it doesn't have an impact on their finances because it doesn't apply. They make their money off of investments, like their business, rental properties, stock and bonds and etc. Capital Gains! These sources are not subject to the income tax assessment that you keep hearing Democrats chanting about going for the jugular and the Republicans want to cut. And, of course, there is always the concern of how it affects the Middle Class, not the wage earners. Everything is about the Middle Class, who are impacted by income taxes but they still are not the majority spender in the commodity market which is our marketplace, as already demonstrated. We are the big buyer of provisions with restaurants and institutions coming in second. We are the majority buyers of the can openers, toasters, coffee pots, TV's and radios. We are the primary buyer of clothing and school supplies and cars and garden tools and literally millions of other items the household uses in its every day experience and survival needs. That is the commoner's economy and we are the market demand that everybody should be concerned about but are clueless about financing it through the time clock.

Business and industry has a bad habit of trying to fatten their profit margins off the backs of labor instead of productivity. With that being said, we are facing another negative impact. Business and industry is becoming more and more automated every day to cut labor costs and improve productivity. That automation is doing more than boosting productivity, it is displacing employees and that has a negative impact on the market, both markets, because it just adds to the unemployment rolls which means less influx of cash into the commoner's economy, (suppression of cash flow). People that are unemployed don't have money to spend and if they don't have money to spend then they can't create market demand. That's what makes conservatives that mock our concerns over displacement look like uncaring low-lifes!

Organized labor is constantly demanding higher and higher wages while preaching to their members that the higher wages is the answer to their financial woes. That is a half truth! We, as individuals, are in business for ourselves. Our product is our skill and labor and those two elements are a commodity. They are a commodity that we are selling to the employer. The cost of all commodities get computed into the final cost of the end product and then the manufacturer applies his/her profit margin onto that to arrive at the price you're going to pay at the cash register and so you end up reimbursing the boss for what he/she is paying you plus interest. The pay raises are only good for however long it takes for the cash register to catch up with the time clock. In the mean time, the rest of the community isn't getting wages to keep up with the cost of the inflation that you created with your pay raise and so your actions impose hardships on the rest of the community. And then you, the union member, wonder why so many of the community despise you because of your demands. The union is a nuisance to the employer but a hardship for the rest of the community.

On the other hand, business and industry has proven time and again that it doesn't have the employee's back and that's the incentive for organizing unions in the first place. The job market is full of people vying to fill common labor positions and so the commoner has no leverage to negotiate a labor agreement or hire a lawyer to enforce one even if he/she did manage to get one. That is why we need the union. Businesses, and that includes government as an employer, regularly renege on their word on benefits and wages. Unless you've got them nailed down by a contract and a way to enforce that contract, then you have nothing to protect your rights. What the union refuses to accept is that wages are a commodity and as such, its cost elevates the costs at the cash register thereby increasing the wage gap that kills the economy overall and eventually shuts down the union business just like everybody else's.

There has to be a financial balance between the time clock and the cash register that can sustain the survival of the commoner and perhaps provide a quality of life that is acceptable but that translates to smaller profit margins for Corporate America and you know how that's going to go over! Most commoners are content with a commoner's kind of lifestyle and aren't especially looking to get rich, especially off their limited skills. Of course, I don't think any of us are going to turn down wealth if it happens to come our way. Yea Lotto! We need to get back to where a single income can sustain the family and where part time jobs are used to get ahead, not sustain the family. Today's financial situation is not an improvement over what we had in the 50's and before then, in spite of what the politicians and guru's of finance espouse on the news. They like to talk about adjusting for inflation, etc., and that we're making more than our parents or grandparents did and a bunch of other BS. All I know is that the percentage of money I have in my pocket after the bills is in the negative and that is with holding down multiple jobs and neglecting the family instead of just one full time job. That's BS!

Some employers, (low wage employers), have share-earning programs that provide a retirement income and an extra income during their employment which helps to make up for shortfalls. Profit sharing is another program that can boost an income. The reason these help is because they come off the profit end of the budget instead of the cost end of the budget for the employer and so your cost doesn't get added into the cost of the commodities used to produce the product.

We used to have overtime but when the labor unions petitioned for the 40-hour work week with overtime for all time worked over the 40, business and industry immediately began paring down the full time positions and replacing them with part time positions. In addition to eliminating the possibility of overtime, they reaped the windfall benefit of not having to provide benefits to the part timers. Naturally, those windfall benefits did not find their way into our paychecks! Of course this impacted the marketplace and market demand because everybody's paychecks went into the toilet and subsequently, so did the economy! We went into a recession until we adjusted to the shafting we got and we are still suffering from the way business and industry did us to fatten their profits at our expense in total disregard for what they would do to the economy and market demand. If business and industry doesn't do something to improve the influx of cash into the economy on a per-capita basis, via the commoner, then we are going to have more economic crashes and economic failures for business and industry and going automated isn't going to help. (If people are unemployed and don't have money, then where's the market demand to justify production?) Its going to aggravate the problem by suppressing market demand even more. We might have to have government assess a fee on companies for the automation that displaces employees and establish a government issued base wage for the general public to make up for the economic losses caused by the automation. When a machine can replace 20 or 30 employees there's no re-education that you can take to fill the positions that no longer exist. That's like telling a thousand employees that if they want better pay then move up the ladder; like one thousand employees can move up and sit at the boss's desk and draw his pay! That was probably one of the stupidest comments a media pundit has ever made!

The company can't possibly pay more than what it charges for its product or service. The product or service has to be able to pay for itself and all the costs associated with production and still turn a profit for the business, giving it a reason to exist!

The point to all of this is that if business and industry cannot fix this problem then it is going to energize the socialist movement in this country even more and they, (the socialists), will impose the solution.

The conversation above is obviously an overview of what is going on in our lives and the use of the word "you" is in reference to America's labor force, more specifically those who punch a time clock or an equivalent pay status. The cost-of-living is what it takes to pay for one's survival without such amenities as vacations or luxury items like investments, fancy new cars, eating out, or living in a fancy hotel or something. It's just the basic needs of food, clothing and shelter and doesn't take into account the cost of unplanned expenses like medical attention for accidents and illness or unforeseen legal expenses. As for the worker not being able to buy the product he or she produces, it should be pretty obvious that the worker at Boeing isn't going to be able to take his or her paycheck and go down to the airplane lot and buy a 747 but the dock worker unloading bananas should be able to go buy a bunch of bananas with his check. So the marketplace spoken of isn't Wall Street or an aircraft catalog; it's a place like a department store, grocery store or filling station, the kind of places we peons are pretty much limited to financially. The point, is that the socioeconomic algorithm exists and works as pointed out. All the hyperbole that we get hit with by Corporate America and the politicians is all smoke and mirrors to keep the natives manipulable for political and financial reasons. A light bulb should go off in our head when we have to pinch pennies to make ends meet and have to rob Peter to pay Paul in order to make the budget work and the politicians keep singing about how great things are. The top two tiers can retire with ease but the working class/common labor is lucky if they can finagle a retirement and even if they can, you can bet they won't be kicking back and sipping margaritas. In today's economic atmosphere, a lot of us are having to find additional means of earning a living in an effort to meet the cost-of-living, especially when family moves back in with you because they can't make it on their own with the paychecks they bring home. All of this causes us to look to government for some answers and of course the politicians want to provide those answers in order to keep us happy so they can keep their jobs and accompanying prestige and benefits. The more the government takes on, the less free we become as we become beholding to it for its redistribution of wealth. Redistribution of wealth should be occurring at the time clock, not the welfare office! The economy requires a sufficient influx of cash on a steady basis to remain healthy. Unemployment stifles that influx and so government has to step in and provide the influx to the commoner that is needed to keep the base economy afloat! Conservatives call this "tax and spend" and "redistribution of wealth" and for the life of them, can't figure out why it's so necessary! For every dollar Corporate America stuffs in its pocket to the detriment of the commoner, government has to collect three; one to replace the loss and two to pay for the collection and redistribution of wealth.

There is a disproportionate distribution of wealth in this country and it is being caused by greed which brings its own karma with it. As I pointed out before, before the 60's, for the most part, families were supported by only one income source. At least that's the way it was for the majority! The one paycheck met the Commoner's cost-of-living, maybe even with a little left over. If we wanted more than that, then we went out and did odd jobs or got a part time job. Odd jobs and part time jobs were not needed to break even. It wasn't us that changed during the twentieth century, it was Corporate America and "its" marketplace. Prior to WWII, women were not a significant part of America's labor force. Most were stay-at-home moms or would be employed at the bank or library, or as a school teacher; fairly safe, unassuming occupations. During the war America's labor force was off fighting the war which made America's labor force a bit devoid of manpower and so business and industry recruited women to fill the empty slots. True to form, Corporate America immediately began to exploit them and take advantage of their complacency and ignorance. They were paid a sub-standard wage on the theory that they were not physically fit, like the men, nor knowledgeable and were therefore a sub-standard asset to the company. After the women proved to be not only as productive as the men but even surpassed their performance, business and industry told them that they needed to keep the pay low because of the war effort. After the war, they continued to exploit the women for sub-standard wages and fattened their bottom line on their backs and to their detriment. On top of that, sexual harassment became a public issue and a common malfeasance within the corporate structure which caused a public revolt towards their behavior and incited the "women's movement!" The Democrats quickly took up this banner while Republicans made fun of it, which was to their detriment!

Prior to WWII, the man was king of his castle and was the family's financial officer. If mama needed money for something she had to hit up dear old dad for it and if he was an #hole, she would probably have to beg for it and then still probably wouldn't get it. When she entered the workforce, bringing home the bacon for herself allowed her to feel what financial freedom was all about and after the war a lot of the women remained in the workforce and opened the corporate doors to include women as a part of America's labor force.

This was one of many socioeconomic and cultural changes that this nation was going through during the twentieth century. After the war, throughout the 50's, households started to become duo income households; not to meet the cost-of-living but to get ahead and be able to afford to own their own home or drive a new car or put towards investments or college for their kids or themselves. They were elevating the status of the Commoner to be more "Middle Class" in quality of life! The second income wasn't necessary for survival, it was an option. By the 60's, Corporate America decided that the two income household could afford a jack in the price of goods and began to inflate the prices of their goods and services. (This too, became a point of contention in the media!) This generated unprecedented inflation in our economy and created a change in the situation to where the second income was now a necessity instead of an option. That was not an improvement in the economy as the politicians were preaching during their campaigns. Their actions was the predecessor to a recession that sent Wall Street into a panic which caused them to install all kinds of bells and whistles to shut down trading if the market began to take a plunge again like it did for the Great Depression. Not one of them got the message! Not one of them, corporate or political, got the message that they were creating an imbalance in our socioeconomic distribution of wealth that was going to cause us problems. They all just kept their hands in the cookie jar and ignored the socioeconomic evolution that the twentieth century was laying on us and ignored the symbiotic relationship that had come to exist between business and labor because of changes in our economy's dynamics as we all chased the brass ring of "progress".

Before WWII and even into the 50's, maybe even the 60's, the majority of us were at least semi dependent on the land and nature for our survival. It supplemented the shortfalls of our commercially generated incomes. Prior to that, we survived off the land and nature and didn't have to depend on currency for our survival. Our currency was commodities and the printed currency was "representative" type currency. It was a certificate of ownership of a specific amount of gold or silver and that gave it real value. When Nixon took us off the Gold standard he collected all the representative currency and replaced it with "fiat" currency, which is nothing more than an IOU whose ethereal value is based on our ability to produce goods and services for the bearer of the note. Guess what? Business and industry left town! What do we back those IOU's with now? Now you're getting the picture of what the trade deficit is really about. We are in the negative in being able to cover all those IOU's if we're called on them! We owe so much money today that we can't even make the payments on our debt. That's called the deficit! The foreign holders of those markers are going to want satisfaction for everything they sold to us and got an IOU for instead of valuable commodities. We've painted ourselves into a corner. At the national level, you don't get to declare bankruptcy and walk away. All nations are interdependent upon one another and when a nation fails, there's a problem. That's one of the reasons you see so much poverty around the world and civil unrest and rebellions. Everybody is fed up with the suffering that bad natural conditions, bad industrial conditions and bad political conditions have levied on them. It's the Devil's brew!

In most governments, the power comes from the top down because of conquest. The leadership took over their country by force and imposed its will upon the people. The only voice the people have is whatever it takes to placate the people and keep a lid on any unrest that develops. In our case, it's just the opposite. In our case, "We the People" are the power, (government by the consent of the governed), and that creates a unique situation. If we are not careful, government can become the firing squad and we get to shout "fire" as we stand in front of it. We need to be vigilant about how we govern ourselves and to whom or what we give the rifles to! We have the ability to remove tyrants without civil war but the tyrants shouldn't have been able to get into position in the first place. "Character Matters!" "Character" governs behavior and judgment. People of bad character do bad things. Pretty simple math, don't you think? Another unique thing about government by the consent of the governed is that the people elected reflect, or are supposed to reflect, the character and values of the people that elected them.

I find it disturbing when a voter calls up a radio station and praises her representative for being a better liar and deceiver than anybody else on Capitol Hill. What does that say about the character of those that elected him and what does that say about the character of this nation? It defames us on an international level! Washington, DC is the face of America and what it does represents what kind of people we are and when we take pride in a politician for being the best at lying, what does that label us as individuals? That is how low we've become morally, intellectually and ethically and that defines who and what we are. That is the type of character the world is forced to see and that affects how they deal with us in all matters and whether they can trust us or not. You can't trust a liar or a thief! Why would you take pride in being labeled a liar and a thief? That caller needs to do a self assessment and so do the voters that elected that person. Many years ago, a certain politician committed murder so she could get elected. She eliminated the opposition! What does that say about the character of the people that were supporting her? We must be introspective about our own character and our ability to judge the character of the people we ask, (by vote), to govern us.

CHAPTER IV

This Commoner's Thoughts about God! -

I consider myself a Christian but unlike others, I do a lot of thinking outside the box. Religions, in and of themselves, tend to be a figment of the imagination and full of superstitions. Plausibility is one of my guiding factors! You cannot deny science! At least if you keep everything in context you cannot deny it! We tend to latch onto theories as absolute facts. Einstein's theory of relativity formula works but has its limitations and that's what keeps it a theory. At least that is what some physicists are claiming. I'm not into complicated formulas and math and so I'll have to leave those judgments up to them!

Darwin's Theory of Evolution has validity to it but like Einstein's Theory, it's got a few hiccups too and so it remains a theory as well. The Bible says, .. "... God Created ..." but it doesn't go into details about how He did it and the timing cited in the Bible is open for debate because the time cited is in earth time, not universe time and it's in earth time because the scriptures were being written by an earth person for earth people, not the universe! The authors of the various scriptures might have been inspired of God, or not, but the authors, beyond a doubt, are flawed human beings that are very capable of screwing things up. God has been in the making for billions of years and so His concept of a day is going to be quite different from ours. At least that's my opinion! (And this is assuming that God began with our universe's beginning and not taking into account that He might have existed before our "Big Bang!")

Science says that all life began in the primordial soup, (prehistoric mud), of the newly formed earth as it was cooling down and beginning to develop the elements we recognize today as planet earth. The Bible says God spit into a pile of dust and made some mud and created man from that mud, (primordial soup?). I think the one just might vet the other!

Science embraces the "Big Bang Theory" and figures that the universe we perceive all came from a burst of energy, (a spark), or a vast array of energies, I should say. Some of those energies were attracted to each other and congealed to form the matter that we recognize as the world and universe around us. Those energies are in the minority. The vast majority of energies emanating from that burst are still unaccounted for and unexplained, like "dark matter", string theory and the Bose particle, to name a few.

Applying Darwin's Theory of Evolution to the evolution of matter and the probability that energy began to congeal and evolve into other forms right out the starting gate, I have to assume that the energies that define life and cognizance had to have begun in that instant as well. Matter is a perception! It has to be! If everything is energy in a vast array of different forms then all matter is still energy and that means that we are energy as well. That makes us energy perceiving energy as matter and/or other energies. When we breakdown matter it gives off energy so that vets the theory that we and all other matter is energy, even if we perceive it as a solid, gas or liquid.

Our five senses are receptors of various forms of energy and our brain interprets the energy they receive as something we can relate to, thereby creating a perception. Our eyes are receptors for light wave energy. Different cones and rods are frequency/duration sensitive, (putting things simply), and so the energies coming into the eyes are like a Morse Code to the brain, which assigns values to those codes that we perceive as colors and objects. Our ears are pressure sensors. The sounds we hear are pulses of air that are received like a Morse Code which gets interpreted in the brain as sound and is given values that we can associate with previous experiences. Touch involves pressure sensitivity and thermal sensitivity, both of which are forms of energy in motion. Taste and smell are ionic sensors that sense the ionic content of matter touching them and is able to assign values to those detections that we recognize as flavors and odors. It is all energy interactions. Our sense of pain is actually thermal as it senses the energy released as the matter that makes up tissue is damaged and releases its energy. The natural electrical currents that race throughout our bodies carrying information back and forth to the brain is energy. We burn energy to stay alive and mobile.

Our brain is nothing more than an organic computer that operates at the atomic level of energy relationships; something that science is just now getting into where computers are concerned. We now have computers that can process terabytes of information per second and yet our minds are capable of much more. We're just inept! The point I'm trying to make is that all of this is evolving energies! It is my presumption that this same kind of development was occurring the second the "Big Bang" began and if the energies that are us could evolve from an energy formed as a humanoid swinging from trees and peeling bananas to one exploring space in a couple million years then how much more could those first energies from the Big Bang have developed with billions of years to work with? If you apply our intellectual timeline for our rate of development to the billions of years that energy was congealing and shaping before we came along then I don't see how anybody could possibly argue against the notion that a living-form of energy began evolving within the first million or so years after the Big Bang and that that energy could very well be the totality of all the energies of the universe and could have developed cognizance within the first two million years after the Big Bang. That energy would be so much more advanced than anything in the universe, especially man, that it has earned the title of God and deserves the title of God, especially since it obviously has full power over whether we exist today or go extinct tomorrow! Because we are human, we assign human values to the image of God and how we expect Him to perform. I don't envision God as a human creature. I don't deny that He might have taken on a human shape as a matter of relevance for us, but I sincerely believe that He is much, much more than that and that His powers and intellect is beyond our two million year old ability to comprehend. He is beyond our conception as an entity. If He is an evolution of the forces of the universe then He is indeed what He says He is, Alpha and Omega, the Beginning and the End! When He goes, we all go! That will be the end and everything will become as though it never was. That is the God that I believe in! A God without limitations!

As for the Bible, I believe in its narrative but I also have to take into account the flawed nature of man and the obvious flawed nature of the authors of the scriptures and the flawed nature of those who interpreted their writings and then decided what would be included and what would be excluded, like the Book of Enoch or the Chronicles of Lilith or the Gnostics. The King James, the forerunner to all the subsequent versions, was interpreted by and compiled by the very same people that persecuted people for believing that the earth is round and that it wasn't the center of the universe. They are the people that orchestrated the Inquisitions which involved false accusations, torture and murder and other heinous crimes against humanity. I'm sorry but that's not exactly what I would look for as being credentials of credibility even if they were "inspired of God!" I would also point out that "inspired of God" is man's opinion. God didn't come down out of the blue and make any such declaration! It's all on us! The way I look at it, they might have been inspired of God but we are also God's version of Murphy's Law! If there's a way to screw things up, He can count on us! It seems that I remember those same people coming to the conclusion that their first translation wasn't totally accurate and so the Bible has been rewritten several times since then. Murphy's Law?

There are two forces throughout the universe and they are either positive or negative. Within the laws of physics we can see them in action in the way that magnets react to each other and in Chemistry in how atomic valences interact with each other. There is one law of physics that applies to all things and it's called "cause and effect!" The cause can be either positive or negative and the effect can be either positive or negative but none the less, that law is going to play out. That law applies to everything from chemical and nuclear reactions to life and social interactions. Bad attitudes generally evoke bad attitudes and vibrant attitudes generally evoke vibrant attitudes. Cause and effect!

Force is the product of energy applied and so all forces come from an energy source of some kind. There are 118 natural elements and a spattering of man made elements, that I'm sure exist somewhere in the universe as a natural element. All of these elements have different characteristics but are subject to the same laws of physics and react the same way to those laws. They are all a convergence of the Hydrogen atom. Molecules are made up of atoms that cling to each other because of their valences. Atoms, on the other hand, are a convergence of Hydrogen atoms. Instead of just clinging to each other, they merge to form new elements. Ie: two Hydrogen atoms merge to form a Helium atom, etc. Nothing is flaked off. The Helium attains two protons, two neutrons and two electrons. As Hydrogen atoms continue to merge, they increase the mass of the atom but the electron shell's outer orbits change in strength as the electron count changes and it gets farther and farther from the core. This changes the character of the resultant atom and how it interacts with other elements.

These elements make up the entirety of the universe that we perceive. Not one of those elements, by itself or collectively, in any configuration has or attains the characteristic of living matter. None of them! Therefore, the conclusion would be that whatever gives inanimate matter the characteristics of living matter has to be a separate energy totally unassociated with the structural or physical dynamics of any of the elements of the Periodic Tables. It is its own entity and it is an energy that exercises all the characteristics of a life form! It has too or whatever it gives life too wouldn't assume life as we recognize it! It has the unique characteristic of being able to be invoked only by another living energy. Only the living can reproduce the living. Chemistry and physics cannot do it! Maybe someday somebody will figure it out but I'm not holding my breath. This is a life-force energy that can only be reproduced by another life-force energy, whether it is plant or animal. When a person dies, we can open up the skull and stimulate the brain with electrical pulses that can cause it to animate different parts of the body but whatever was running that organic computer is long gone and is no longer running the show. The fact that we can animate the body through electrical impulses suggests that the life-force energy was producing the same stimulations to produce animation and interactions and if that's the case then that proves that that life-force energy is a living entity capable of cognizance, rationalizing and determinations because it is determining which buttons to push to make the body act like a living, interacting human being. When it's gone, the body returns to being an inanimate pile of the inanimate elements that it was made from. "Dust thou art and unto dust thou shalt return!" Very Biblical!

I try to apply common sense to my reasonings and embrace what appears to me to be logical and therefore truthful. When somebody tries to convince me that something is the truth then red flags go up all over the place because "truth" stands on its own merits. Why the extra effort to convince me that something is the truth when the truth can stand on its own merits? I'm not trying to convince you that I'm telling the truth but I am asking that you think about it and draw your own conclusions through logic.

I look at the Old Testament as a kind of diary of human society and the etiology of how humanity has evolved over the millennia. Obviously, Moses wasn't around for the beginning of creation or the Great Flood. It is assumed that it was he that penned the Book of Genesis! There are other ancient texts much older than the Book of Genesis that also tell of creation and the Great Flood and so I imagine that Moses was probably a learned person in addition to being close to God. I have to take into account the probability that there were a few things lost in the translations from these ancient scrolls, not only because the ancient Hebrew language was extinct by the time the scrolls were found, but because the scrolls were in pretty bad shape with large portions dissolved by age so that they appeared like moth eaten fragments of a document. Couple that with the fallibilities of man and we have reasonable doubt about consistency of text and the probability that a lot of literary license was taken with the composing of their stories. Nonetheless, the narrative throughout its context is consistent even though none of the original authors had a clue about the other's existence. Some influence spanned the gaps in time and distance between writings so as to produce a consistency of narrative. This gives pause to the probability that God exists and that He was indeed inspiring the penning of the records passed down through the ages thus, "scriptures inspired of God". Man is the only fly in the ointment and as for "inspired of God", that's man's opinion; God hasn't shown up and declared that to be the case. (Just for the record, God's not in the habit of doing stage performances for validations. He talks to us by means of the spirit – living energy!)

We learn from history and we learn from our mistakes and our achievements. That cannot be argued! When pride, ego or negligence interferes with that learning process, bad things happen! We become prone to repeating the screw-ups that we read about, or failed to read about and we repeat history while always getting the same results. It's insane that we keep doing this! When you couple this with our impetuous nature, we tend to compound the consequences. We need to shape up!

The Old Testament is a testimonial about how we've evolved over the centuries. It is a testimonial about how we came to believe in the things that we believe and how we arrived at what was moral and what was not and why. Why would you challenge the veracity of the scriptures and skip over the lessons they were trying to convey? At the very least, they serve as parables which still apply to this day. We still practice most of the lessons conveyed by them. We have the Book of Psalms which is a collection of prose and poems that produces a movement of the spirit within us in the same way that we listen to today's music and poetry and other writings to sooth the soul or accent a story or movie. And there's the Book of Proverbs which espouses quips and quotes about dealing with life's contests and our emotions. It's contents do not have to be courtroom evidence quality. It's suggestive! As for many of the prophesies here and there, you don't have to be prophetic or clairvoyant to perceive what's coming down the pike when society is pursuing a set course in life thru its cultural evolution and pursuits. You don't have to be Edgar Casey to know that something bad is going to happen when society keeps beating on a hornet's nest with a short stick!

Just a thought; I'm not overly convinced about the ability to see into the future via clairvoyance. I think that our subconscience probably picks up on all kinds of information from all around us 24/7 and in some people, the subconscience organizes all that information and extrapolates where we are headed under the conditions currently known. Global Warming, which is full of a lot of misinformation, is one of those extrapolations. None of these gurus of science can explain why every planet in the solar system is warming up concurrently and at the same ratios, proportionate to size and distance from the sun, as is the earth. There's no doubt that our habits are going to be contributing something to how our environment is going to evolve but we also have to accept the fact that nature is going to do its own thing just as it has done for millions of years, with or without us. We need to learn to adapt or die! We are the only creature on earth that has the ability to manipulate the outcome! On the other hand, this is the only home we have and we have no business turning it into a garbage dump, which is never healthy! Because of our intellect, we are the natural caretakers of the earth and we need not be derelict in our responsibilities.

Oops, getting off track!

I find the New Testament much more viable. Its information and accountings are verifiable because there was fairly accurate record keeping in place during its events which vets the testimonies given within its books. Some people just flat out choose not to accept anything as fact or truth, no matter who is doing the talking or what the topic is and so denial of the scriptures is a piece of cake for them, which is going to be to their detriment in the end, not that they can comprehend a reason to care.

To understand what the New Testament is about, we have to go back to the Old Testament and the story of Adam and Eve. Adam and Eve might have been real people, (I wasn't there so I don't know), but in my opinion, they were a metaphor for humanity. I can say that because they were not alone on this planet as many people automatically think. Following the testimony, Adam and Eve started out with two kids, Cain and Able. Cain murdered Able and was ostracized from the family. Cain made pleadings to God for some protection from being murdered himself for what he had done. Who was going to murder him if Adam and Eve were the only people around and they already demonstrated that they weren't going that route? Why did he need "the Mark of Cain" upon his forehead? God granted him his wish and guess what? He hooked up with another tribe of people and then immigrated to even another tribe of people. Meanwhile, Adam & Eve were still just two. Where did all the other people come from and why would they be prone to murdering him for what he had done if Adam and company were all alone? How in the world would they have known about it, unless Adam and Eve were leaders of the population, unrelated, of those days? I deduce that they were probably leaders and therefore were metaphors also, for how all of humanity was behaving in those days. That's why when God severed ties with them and cast them out just like they did Cain, and cursed them, it applied to all of humanity. The only other game in town was Lucifer and apparently he gladly took us in, if for no other reason, just to irk God and get in his digs for God having ditched him. Logical? Technically, we became the spawn of Satan and so our character and behavior is very much impacted by his character and behavior in much the same way that we tend to mimic the character and behavior of the parents that raise us. The wages of sin is death; all sins! That is the curse we have to be saved from or we inherit from Satan everything he has coming to him, which is death, after all, we are his heirs. Prior to the fall of Adam and Eve, (humanity), we were God's heirs; a much better position to be in, I think!

The Jews don't call the New Testament the New Testament. They call it the Last Testament as in Last Will and Testament. Our salvation from Satan's penalty is His last will and testament and a will doesn't become active until the testator dies and then its awards are given to the heirs. This is logical, yes? Does it make sense now, why Jesus had to die; and He died willingly so as to bring His will to life and fulfill the legacy He left for us. Now I'm sounding like a Bible Thumper; oh well! It's an important concept! There's a lot of pomp and circumstance assigned to the act of transitioning from sinner to saved, probably because it is deemed to be such an important event in our lives. Repentance is an accepting of the fact that you were born into sin because of the curse and no doubt have pursued behaviors that would be considered sin, especially when motive is brought into the picture. Repentance is recognizing and accepting responsibility for this status and feeling enough remorse over how they've lived their lives, whatever their malfeasances might have been or how slight and make an oath to themselves and to God to denounce that style of life and do their best to live up to God's standards and bring honor to His house and His family. That is called being born again! You're starting a new life under Christ and His teachings and that is being born again. Baptism is an outward declaration of that rebirth. Are we going to screw up again? More than likely! What counts is that it wasn't intentional and we quickly as possible make things right and ask God to please forgive us for our trespasses as we forgive others. Intent is everything! We can't go through life deliberately committing transgressions and expect forgiveness. Deliberately doing wrong is not an example of having repented. No repentance, no forgiveness! Becoming Christians doesn't automatically make us saints and so we have no business sitting in judgment of others. That doesn't mean that we don't recognize others for what they are and not expect it to show up in their behavior. Expecting somebody to follow certain behavior patterns because of who they are is not judgment, it's self defense from being exploited, taken advantage of or even placed in mortal danger. It is also our cue to pray for them and diplomatically witness to them by how we act and live our lives, not run our mouths.

Tolerance is an abused term that wrecks a lot of havoc, especially these days. Tolerance should mean we don't abuse others just because they believe differently than we do. It doesn't mean we allow thugs into our living room to destroy our home. It doesn't mean that we go into theirs to destroy their home either! The inquisitions was a demonstration of intolerance. Intolerance for violators of human rights, as far as I'm concerned, is perfectly acceptable. An intolerance of alternative religions is unacceptable. In other words, we don't set about attacking others for believing differently than we do. Our enticement to become a Christian lies in how we live our lives and how we treat others and intolerance is counter to that goal. People become Christians because they are attracted to the faith and want to live that kind of life; it is not an imposed faith forced upon people against their will as we are seeing under a lot of Islamic practices. We don't use persecution or the threat of persecution to attain or retain our members, such as the Church of Scientology is accused of doing or as the early churches did prior to us abandoning Europe for America. Those that engage in that kind of behavior are false prophets. There are two commandments that Christ issued on how we should behave, "Do unto others as you would have them do unto you" and "Love thy neighbor as thyself"; in other words treat each other as beloved family.

Families can have a "Black Sheep" of the family and they get dealt with according to their behavior but the family still doesn't disown them like Adam and Eve did Cain. We monitor their lives and hope and pray that someday a light bulb will go off in their head and they will see the light and change their ways. We constantly wish and hope for the better and we generally are there with the band aids when they get hurt but not necessarily with a lot of sympathy. A lot of people, especially atheists and other non believers make fun of those who've chosen to live a Christian life, probably because they can't cut the mustard themselves; jealousy! Living a Christian life is a tough road to hoe when you're living in a world of people that champion the efforts of the anti-Christ and like nothing better than to torment you and beat you down and try your faith. Their idea of tolerance is accepting and practicing other people's faiths as a matter of keeping the peace and staying on their good side. That is not tolerance! That's acquiescence! We can be courteous and respectful without bowing to somebody else's god or culture. Some people are just plain evil; like sociopaths and serial killers. I'd have a problem remaining the "nice guy" when it comes to one of them. We have others among us that are just plain evil and constantly act out towards other people; family and drugs and alcohol tend to present them at their worse and amp up their negative behavior, even to the point of violence. From rocking chair observation, (non-scientific observation), I would suspect that many of these people are prone to suicide when their conscience catches up to them and they realize they need to change and find that they can't do it alone. These people need serious prayer from the secrecy of our room, not through some sort of side show! The miracle of life is when you see the changes happen and only you and God know you prayed.

There was an unscientific experiment done by a rather famous night time talk show host whose shows generally involve stories of paranormal events, UFO's, etc. He, and some of us followers, were curious about the power of our minds within the realm of telepathy and prayer. He had some associates that he knew, that lived in rather remote or off-beat regions of the world and he recruited them to participate in his little research project. He had them find locations where they could be completely off-grid and isolated from radio, TV, phone service or a power grid. He then had them take energy measurements in those locales to use for a baseline for the project. He then gave them a specific day/night time to be at each of their locations and he coordinated that time with the time for initiating the experiment over the airwaves. He had all his listeners focus their thoughts and prayers on one specific location near the tip of South America. He then checked back with his volunteers to see how their readings went during the broadcast time frame. Everybody had normal readings except the one located at the tip of South America. His energy readings nearly doubled over the time frame of the experiment. The conclusion that he, and I, got was that the accumulative energies of the mind do travel great distances and therefore have a high probability for having an affect on a target. It might not be much but there's a connection none the less! Energy was being sent from our collective being to that spot where it became evident!

If this worked under conditions which were measurable then I am most certain that our prayers to God and Christ are being transmitted and received even if our conversation is a bit one-sided. We just have to have faith that we are making a connection and that He is listening!

This validation of mental telepathy should be taken seriously by those who like to play Satanic games and engage in Satanic rituals. That realm is not something to toy with because the intended targets are not harmless or complacent mortals. They are not restricted by the codes of Christianity or God and therefore have no morals, ethics or any other kind of social limitations that would apply to them or what they want to do. You, because of your naivety, are their target and they can use you to get at God and that makes you very expendable and not their friend, even in the slightest way!

You've got to remember that the matter that makes up your body has no life-force energy of its own. (Remember what I pointed out about the 118 natural elements!) Its energy comes from you as an energy being, a soul. You are the owner/operator of your body and the life-force energy that is you is what we call a soul or spirit. When your soul leaves the body, it is the body that dies and quits operating and if left to nature, returns to the basic elements from which it was made. Getting a little into the world of the paranormal and fantasy, the demons of the occult are of this same life-force energy and are just as unrestricted by material things as you have become after leaving the body and that makes them lethal and something to be respected for the dangers they pose. They can take up residence in your body right along with you and drive you nuts! If you have a countenance that invites them into your life, they will oblige. That's why I advise not toying with the occult as though it is some sort of harmless game or just superstition. It is a serious misadventure going there! To be a Christian, you have to be a believer; to be a victim of the occult, you don't have to believe in anything because you're an empty vessel just waiting for occupancy. I'm not talking Bible here; I'm talking science and theory, even if I am using the jargon of the occult and religion.

When we talk about spirit, it is generally in reference to how we approach life or some task. In the religious sense, it is reference to the type of spirit we allow to guide us in our approach to life, thus we have evil spirited people like the sociopath and we have the righteous or right spirited people like Mother Teresa or other unsung heroes who go about the world doing good without any accolades. It's hard to figure out why some people find that their passion in life is to screw up other people's day as opposed to others who can only see the good or the spiritual needs of others, justified or not. As Christians, we have invited God's Holy Spirit, (the energy that has been evolving since the beginning), into our lives as our co-pilot, with the intent of using our lives to be a blessing to ourselves and to all others. Demon worshipers invite evil into their lives to accent the evil desires that they already embrace and it isn't to do right by others, it is to do evil towards others and even to themselves. As far as I'm concerned, they've got some mental issues if they're wanting to take that direction in life, demons or not, devil or not!

Mixing the carnal with the spiritual and really thinking outside the box, I think that the soul, (living energy), initially requires the flesh, (plant or animal), to propagate more souls. The body acts like a sort of nursery that the soul uses to interact with other beings and creatures to learn about life and life's values and to use to produce more souls. Now I'm sounding like Carl Sagan and one of his space fantasies! Some people go through life and for some reason never develop spiritually while others develop considerably, to the point of becoming ministers, mystics, psychics and so on. Becoming spiritually aware would be pretty good preparation for when we part company with our body and become a spiritual being instead of a carnal being.

The point I'm trying to make is that living matter does not exist because of the chemical or mechanical properties of what we are made of. The force that turns the inanimate material that we are made of into a living creature is a completely separate force that does not exist within the context of the elements of the Periodic Table or the laws of physics and that puts the characteristics of life into a realm all its own with its own laws of physics that can, and sometimes does, interact with the carnal world that we except as our universe. It is this interaction and its properties that we call "paranormal". There is nothing superstitious about it or, in context, abnormal. It is simply an alternate energy that science cannot explain any better than it can explain all the other forces unaccounted for in the universe, which surpasses by far what we can explain.

I'm coming to the conclusion that living matter exists to perpetuate living energy entities because it cannot be produced by any other means. Life has to come from life! All biological forms exist for the sole purpose of creating and nurturing life-force energy beings, (souls), and our biological form serves as a cocoon until either it becomes unviable and unable to sustain itself or the energy-being reaches a certain stage of maturity and has to leave the body, like a butterfly leaves its cocoon to continue its life in another form.

Let's entertain another form of paranormal physics! In the 80's, (I think it was back then), a university decided to engage in an experiment regarding telepathy. In their lab was a good sized aquarium full of Gold Fish or Guppies, or whatever (breeds are of no concern), that were the lab's pets. They were fed and cared for randomly, on a whenever basis and that made them the perfect subject. Then one day, this idea popped into their heads to test the theory about animals/creatures, having psychic abilities that allowed them to communicate with each other telepathically. They got themselves another aquarium and divided the tank's population between the two aquariums and took the second aquarium to an office at the other end of the facility and set up observation camera's in there so that they could observe their behavior at the same time they were observing the behavior of those in the lab.

What they did next was totally revealing. Whenever somebody walked by the lab tank and tossed in a pinch of food, the fish would go into a feeding frenzy. In the second tank, at the other end of the complex and in total isolation, the fish in the isolated tank went into a feeding frenzy at the same moment even though there was nobody around and nothing being fed to them. Obviously, they were communicating through the use of telepathy. They were totally in tune with each other in spite of the separation. The theorem put forth by some scientists is that humans used to have this same capacity except that our advanced communication skills and technologies eliminated the need for psychic communications and so, as Aristotle said, "that which is not used, wastes away"! We traded off our ability to communicate through telepathy for technology and a physical means of communicating.

Beyond that, take note that the communications were instantaneous. There was no lag time in their communication and so guess what? That makes the communication faster than the speed of light or electricity. The next question should be, "what medium is this communication using that is outside the limitations of the laws of physics as we know them?"

Beginning in the 40's, (during WWII), we, and other nations, including our enemies, were engaging in this psychic phenomena, telepathy. We all were experimenting with what became known as "Remote Viewing!" Like with the fish, the psychic and the target were completely separated from each other with the psychic left completely in the dark about the subject target. The clocks at both sites were synchronized to validate the interactions between the reading and the activities to be observed. I think the score rate was at around 50%, which is very much beyond random coincidence. In the cases where there was a valid hit, the time observed by the observer was in perfect sync with the target and the lab. The fact that they got a hit was a validation of the hypothesis but of greater interest to me is what is the medium that this communication took place in? What force was it using? The distance between lab and target was extensive in all cases. In the one, the lab was in England and the other was in Germany. The targets were located in the New England area and the Great Lakes region. It takes time for light to travel that distance, measurable time! In these tests, the communication was instantaneous. The observations were in perfect sync with the validating clocks. That means that the communication was traveling faster than the speed of light. What is the medium that this communication is using that defies our understanding of the law of physics? Keep in mind, these events perfectly parallel the tests with the fish. It blows the theory that the speed of light is the maximum speed that anything can travel out of the water and you can bet that the scientists that embrace that ideology are going to buck the test results because they don't like to be proven wrong, even if they are. This energy medium, like the living energy that is us, are forces that science cannot yet explain or account for. This is the universe of God and religion, and the world of the paranormal. It is unfortunate that so much of the paranormal on display for entertainment purposes is a charade and a deception that corrupts any study of the real deal.

CHAPTER V

The Fall of a Nation -

Culture defines a nation and determines its ultimate destiny. A nation begins under the influence of a founding culture created by the derivatives that inspired its founding, whether it came about via conquest or by self-determination. Our initial culture came about as the result of self-determination and the derivatives that moved us to become an independent nation.

Our founding population was formed by people that were brought up under the imposed influence of Christianity as the social standard. That doesn't mean that everybody was on board with the faith but there's no way they could escape its influence because many of the laws of the land have their basis in the laws spoken of in the Bible, (and which exist in other religious teachings as well). Those who initially began settling this country brought those traditions, values and respects to this country because they were hammered into them by how they were raised, for better or for worse. That's why most of us say that we were founded as a Christian Nation! It wasn't because we canonized Christianity into law and established our government as a sectarian form of government; it was because we reflected the Christian culture in general and displayed Christian behavior and respect in our everyday life and therefore its influence in governance was inevitable. It was an influence, not a mandate!

While on the topic of government and church, churches are not taxed because then the church would be participating in the financing of our government and its many unholy alliances and endeavors and that buys them a stake in what our government does; this is why we have separation of church and so the one cannot dominate over the other except by the will of the majority. The Supreme Court ruled that labor unions could not use their general revenues, (coming from membership dues), for political endeavors because a conflict of interest arises out of the fact that not all members are of the same political persuasions. The entities of government endorse and sponsor politically motivated endeavors, including the supporting of candidates, and the church's detractors have already voiced their opposition to that on numerous occasions. They demand separation of church and state and therefore the church cannot be contributing to government! If it has to contribute to government then the gloves come off and it cannot be obstructed from pursuing political agendas or be ostracized from participation in political affairs. Government endorses abortions; most churches oppose abortions. It would be illegal and improper for church taxes to be used for such endeavors as a conflict of interest would arise because of a church's now mandated contribution (taxes), in a similar fashion as union dues.

All our founders were Christians of some sort and so were most all of those who championed our independence; just not all of us were practicing Christians. Just like today, many of us are Christians, just not practicing Christians; in other words, we're not regulars down at the church or for dancing in the isles. We believe in the value of the Ten Commandments and believe in the declarations of the New Testament as it defines how we should live our lives and approach our trials and tribulations.

This is an important distinction because it defined our way of life and established a culture that was beneficial to our growth and prosperity as a nation; a culture that much of today's society has abandoned or downright desecrated. In concert with this decline of cultural integrity, our prosperity and influence as a nation has declined proportionately.

There's an old observation that states that as soon as we are born we start our journey to death. We are born to die! Apparently, this applies to nations as well! Nations have come and gone all around the world since the beginning of man! They all pass because of cultural decline or conquest, (usually brought on because of cultural decline; predators can smell the blood in the water), or both. We had dissension even before the Declaration of Independence was agreed too and signed. The one side believed that all men are created equal and with that being said, believed that nobody had a right to rule over anybody else, (equals, not subordinates), unless they have that person's consent.

The other side of the argument disagreed. The other side believed that they were destined to rule over others because of the social status that they were born into, their wealth and their superior intellect, (their opinion). Those are the Old School standards of the homelands from which they immigrated, ie: because of the oppression that that ideology imposed upon them.

Now, why would you think that that kind of thinking is good if you already had to flee from its oppression?

None the less, they held their ground and refused to join the Union unless their right to own slaves was left intact. Their reasonings for dominance constituted their reasonings for enslaving others. In their opinion, the slaves were ignorant and stupid and that's why they got captured and enslaved. Democratic Senator Calhoun reflected as much in his speech to the Senate in February of 1837, supporting the secession of the Confederate States from the Union. The people that embraced this ideology from the days of our founding were the forerunners of the Democratic Party and it was the majority of the Democratic Party that Senator Calhoun represented when he stood before the Senate and made his speech. (The majority of Democrats were from the South.) This history is part of the Congressional Record if you should wish to research it! (For the record, and giving the devil his dues, Senator Calhoun was considered one of the greatest Senators ever!)

After the Civil War, in spite of having lost it, the Democratic Party, (mostly of the South), had the audacity to petition Congress for the return of all slaves to their rightful owners as part of the South's

Reconstruction Act! The Party championed segregation across the nation, separate but equal status and championed the Jim Crow Laws, which they authored. The Party still embraces the ideology that other people should kow-tow to their opinions because of their superior intellect, social status and wealth. This ideology was reiterated in 2008, 2009 and 2010 when leaders of the Democratic Party expressed it by calling their constituents, "Low Information Voters", which is code for "ignorant", and blatantly and publicly, some of their leadership flat out called all voters "stupid"; too stupid to comprehend, let alone vote on, the ACA! Apparently they weren't as smart as they thought they were because their design was engineered to go belly up. They lied about keeping your insurance, lied about keeping your doctor, lied about keeping types of coverage and lied about its financial viability and costs and yet they have a cadre of followers that continue to worship at their feet and refuse to hold them accountable! It is more important to them to be able to hate Republicans than admit the error of their ways and work on a fix! Is worshiping their donkey of such great significance to them that they have no problem falling on their swords in behalf of the lies?

The point is that they still think they are smarter than everybody else and continue to treat the American voter as being beneath them and ignorant and stupid about everything if they are without their dominance and leadership. The point of all arguments and all debates is the litigate's belief that they know the truth and that they have the correct answers. We all contain some knowledge of some kind, or skills that are exclusive to our person and when we hear things that are contrary to our beliefs and/or experiences, we want to counter that opposing belief with our own arguments and, if everything is civil, this opens a dialogue of evaluation and study, and if we're lucky, new discoveries and more information are added to our library of knowledge. It is when we begin to think that we are God's gift to humanity that we get into trouble. Nobody has a corner on the market where knowledge is concerned but there can be no argument that some people are more intellectually endowed than others; but even with that acknowledgment, nobody can know everything about everything and that makes us all intellectually dependent on one another to fill in our own voids. As one would surmise, one's intellect is actually limited to the studies they were exposed to. Nobody inherits a library of knowledge that would warrant all others to acquiesce to them. Therefore, those who think that their "superior intellect" gives them a right to dominate over the lives of others is greatly mistaken.

As for wealth and social status, even the most despotic dictators have that on the people they oppress and that is why our founders designed our government the way they did; so that we could get rid of despots through the voting process instead of insurrection and civil war, with great loss of life and even more oppression. However, they also installed in the Constitution the right for citizens to arm themselves so that they can revolt if the leadership of this country should choose to ignore the Constitution and rule of law to oppress us. Please take note as to which party is advocating the revoking of the current Constitution, citing its age, and pushing for the disarming of all citizens! I know I sound like I really have it in for the Democratic Party but this party has abandoned its loyalty to this country as it champions the desecration of the flag, the abandonment of the Pledge of Allegiance, acts of insurrection and violence against the indigenous government, and engages in blatant acts of treason for political profit, and they publicly boast of these acts as though they can do no wrong. If the party, (either party), dominates Capitol Hill then its members are able to have each other's back no matter how heinous the action and bury the malfeasances of its leadership. This problem is not just germane to the Democrats, it applies to the Republican Party as well for we have all witnessed the malfeasances of both parties without seeing them suffer the consequences for their actions under the law.

In the past, such conduct was more for the gossip pages than it was a threat to the nation and national security but our advances in technology and real time communications has changed the playing field and rewritten the game to be played. In the days of our founders, it took weeks, even months or years, to achieve what we achieve today in a matter of minutes. Negligence and malicious behaviors and decisions reap immediate consequences for this nation internally and on the world stage and it is well acknowledged that fatal errors in judgment can occur in a split second when there's no room for error. That's why we get so concerned over who has their finger on the nuclear button of the White House! Allowing business as usual where politics and government is concerned will be our undoing! It's time to hang up the towel of ignorance and become FULLY knowledgeable about what our elected and appointed leaders are doing and become knowledgeable on the issues under fire. Be forewarned, such a project is labor intensive! Somebody needs to monitor the issues and extrapolate to the extreme what the consequences of our actions will be before we do them, not experience them after the fact! The ACA is case in point! We needed some kind of affordable health care that would be available to everybody but those who concocted the ACA were inept and ignorant about what they were doing, (while caught up in their self assessment of having superior intellect), and ignored the factors that would doom the plan. They chose to wallow in their personal opinion of superior intellect instead of incorporating as much input as possible. Now we have a debacle! Of course the Republican establishment didn't do much to entice an invitation to be involved either. Both parties have become self-serving to the point that they engage in obstructionism, the one against the other and neither party provides for an inclusive environment for the other to participate but which wouldn't participate anyway for fear of appearing as a party member in name only, ie: RINO & DINO, (Republican In Name Only/Democrat In Name Only).

Every society/civilization is maintained by four phenomena, which we call institutions. They are the family, (which is the foundation of civilization), religion, education and community. If any of the four become compromised then that civilization begins to tumble like a house of cards because they are all interdependent. Some cite economics as one of our cornerstones but economics only exists within the environment of "community". If you live off the land as our ancestors did, and as some people are doing today, then economics doesn't exist because you're not engaged in barter at any level, or at least to any degree. Therefore, economics is a product of community but with the understanding that it is just as critical to community as the other institutions are to the existence of civilization and once the other institutions become the cornerstones of "community" they then also become subject to the forces of economics upon the well being of the whole. All these institutions must be protected at all costs if the civilization is going to remain intact and survive.

The family is the anchor of all civilizations because it is what influences the character and nature of each succeeding generation and, after all, it is where civilization began. Compromising its influence on the civilization that each generation of parents gave birth too, is detrimental to the continuity, through its culture, and the stability it imparts on civilization. The hardships of the pioneer life and living off the land often called for the absence of the husband from the household, for the purposes of hunting and trapping as the means of putting food on the table and making clothing), and an absence of his influence, at least in real time. "Just wait until your father gets home" was a pretty popular phrase that all of us feared. The children of these households were subject to a disciplined lifestyle because of the demands of nature towards surviving, with chores, maybe home schooling, (much of which came from using a Bible to teach reading skills). You were strictly taught to respect your elders and community leaders. "Yes Sir" and "No Sir" was expected in all conversation. Mother set the rules and father was the enforcer! The hardships were plenty but the crime rates were nearly zip when you compare their days with today's generations. So what changed from the days of their culture and today's culture? It's in how we raised our kids; or rather, how our parents and their parents raised our generations and taught us how to raise our successors! As our great grandparents, grandparents and parents were raised, values and traditions went to the wayside and were not passed down; leaving each succeeding generation devoid of the values and traditions that were supposed to have been passed down. You cannot pass down to the next generation what was never passed down to you. You can't teach what you've not learned!

This is a marked decline in our culture and it can only get worse because there's nothing there to turn back too. Turning things around will require introspect on each person's part where we examine our own personal values under the lamp of right or wrong, not legally, but morally. Do we start with the approval of little white lies which get progressively worse or do we draw a line and not trespass over that line? When is murder OK? When is cheating on your spouse OK? I say never! These are standards of conduct that are detrimental to the victim's good and welfare and the peace and tranquility of the community in general. Obviously, we would want to avoid making the same mistakes in judgment that rendered bad karma and so we should put those things on our list of "do-nots" and in retrospect, figure out how we should have handled the incident that backfired on us in the end. Aside from the "so and so begat so and so", the Bible is an introspective examination of humanity's conduct during the eras of the authors. It gives names, places and incidents within the context of the events cited. It shares with us their perspective and belief in God and how He interacted with humanity. It isn't just a history lesson, it's a social studies lesson and a civics lesson upon their era of life on this planet. It provides a definitive picture of how the belief in God shaped their personal principles, values and virtues! That's why we should carefully take the Old Testament to heart and look for the irrevocable truths that it contains. Why put ourselves through the same misery they went through when we can just read about their FUBAR's and not do them ourselves?

As cited, religion is one of our cornerstone institutions, despite what the atheist would like to have you believe. In spite of having a secular government, (which is a good thing as it preserves Religious Freedom), the church's influence has a stabilizing impact on the community. The church isn't just the perpetuator of a deity; it is the perpetuator of morals, ethics, values, virtues and traditions that the community as a whole has established as its acceptable standard of conduct and character for the individual and the community.

Religion is a derivative of family. If we take things back to Adam and Eve as being the first family then it is understandable how they passed on to their generations the stories about what God expected of them but more than that, every household begins developing rules of conduct as soon as junior or sis is born. Who takes out the garbage, who changes the diapers, who sets the rules and who enforces them, for example. Who tells the kids to "shut up and sit down and eat your dinner"? Who tells the kids how to play with each other, how to share, how to love? These are all family issues and they transpose into community values as we grow up and begin to employ them in our interactions with the world outside of our homes. It is these values that are invoked into us by our parents and that we embrace as community standards of etiquette and behavior that became the tenets espoused by many of our scriptures and Christ Himself. The interactions between the few that embrace the church, and the majority of the population that makes up the community, is what keeps perpetuating the values found acceptable and which are constantly reiterated in the sermons and teachings of the church. Thus, it adds to community stability and becomes one of the community's cultural anchors.

In the Old Testament, the people lived under the rule of law, laws made up by flawed human beings and influenced by the world they lived in and blinded by personal agendas and political loyalties. The Ten Commandments is the only place where God Himself handed us a basic set of laws by which to live and since we no longer have the tablets, there is no validation of that! Many of man's laws and their consequences were extremely harsh because the laws were driven by the emotions of the offended looking to vent their anger, hatreds and emotions, (revenge), on those that offended them. The New Testament is about living by grace. Christ teaches us to "Love thine neighbor as thyself", "Do unto others as you would have them do unto you" and to have compassion and understanding for others. (If you want to understand how far this kind of behavior will carry you, all you have to do is look at the old mobs. They were vicious beasts in reality but they took care of the people that surrounded them, (neighborhood, not members), and as a result, people protected them with a wall of silence, part out of fear of retaliation and part because the mob was their cash cow and protector.) If we live by Christ's standards then there would be no need for laws and punishments because we would all have each other's backs; judgment then, could be left up to God because only He really knows a person's heart. All our sins and all violations of the law begin in the heart and what's in our heart begins in how we were raised and the kind of company we've allowed ourselves to be influenced by; the company we keep! Now we're back to family values and responsibilities! All ex-cons and all ex-addicts, stress on the prefix "ex", and cops and counselors will tell you that the first thing you need to do to get your life right is to part company with the company you used to keep while your life was all wrong. Change your environment and its influence on your life and you will change your life, unless you're still intent on hanging on too your old values and old ways!

We are subject to an even greater influence in our lives than the company we keep; it's our ever changing culture which has been changing because our society has been changing and not for the better. The rules of life that we observed in the past are no longer being observed religiously. It has gotten to where the only time they're observed is when it works to somebody's advantage politically or financially. I was listening to a radio talk show, back when a certain politician was campaigning for the presidency, when a lady, (a Democrat), called in to the show and started bragging about how her candidate was able to out lie everybody. She was proud that her candidate was a liar! Two politicians, during the initial years of the Obama Administration, committed blatant acts of treason against the United States and got a pass because their peers and their supporters were of no better caliber than those who were in charge of Capitol Hill and involved a Judicial System, that is supposed to be non-partisan and a uniform enforcer of the law, and protector of the Constitution and National Security. When you have the fox guarding the chicken house, who do you go to too protect you from the likes of them? Obviously, a couple of people with no morals or loyalty to this country got elected and were in a position to do whatever they wanted to whomever they wanted because of their position. There's nothing to stop them from abusing their office or power! There was another Representative that got a young man fired from his job simply because he found the kid objectionable. So much for honesty and character! That's just a few examples of how badly some parents have raised the kids that are now a part of America's leadership. This is evidence that our now acceptable, substandard behavior began several generations back. This is representative of the social decline of

American society and subsequently it is reflected in the deterioration of the culture that once kept us safe upon our streets and in our homes and allowed us the freedom and tranquility to prosper. We've gone from being able to sit out on our front porch and enjoy an evening of peace to a culture where if you sit out on the front porch you could get shot in a drive-by! That is a degeneration of American society and its culture! The rules of a civilized society have become optional, not standard. That is social decay and the stench is getting to us all as the rot spreads throughout the barrel.

All of our cornerstones are an evolutionary product of the family unit. Community is a cornerstone because it is the result of families gathering all together where we can support and protect each other as a group, just like wild animals do. Animals form herds and prides, etc., as a matter of security against the predators that would have no problem picking them off if they were off by themselves. We came together as a nation as a matter of self defense against the oppressors that we could not defeat on an individualized basis. Our natural penchant for barter and socialization finds itself right at home in the community environment and that lends to our bonding together as community, which creates a natural curtailing of crime, because of the fostering of a more moral culture and that lends to the "domestic tranquility" that we all desire.

Our degeneration is attributable to the congealing of the "perfect storm" of multiple compromises of our roots/foundation and cornerstones. Remember, the family is our foundation and from that springs the cornerstones of church, community, knowledge and economics, with the church representing the moral base that societies build upon.

Between the end of the Civil War and the early 1920's, we went on an alcohol binge and capped that with the passage of the 18th Amendment, (Prohibition). Alcoholism renders the ability of the family unit to exercise its responsibilities towards family, church and community null and void. Families became dysfunctional and estranged as we entered into WWI which compromised the family influence on the quality of our American culture, though not as badly as the 18th Amendment.

As a nation, we crashed and burned financially, (economic cornerstone), which added to our woes and our dysfunctionality. Then along came WWII which damaged the family structure and its influence on Americana even more. The able bodied men marched off to war and the women took their place in the workforce, leaving their kids estranged to other relatives or babysitters/strangers. Now they learn their social etiquettes and achieve the character and behavior that they will need as adults from somebody other than their parents. After the war, many of the women decided that they liked bringing home the bacon and managing it their own way, and instead of becoming the stay-at-home moms of the past, they chose to pursue careers, putting careers and finances ahead of the kids and family; and macho man wasn't about to don the apron and take her place in the family structure! Some women's husbands and boyfriends didn't make it home from the war and so they were left no choice but to struggle to put bacon on the table.

During the 50's, the transition in our culture from being a stay-at-home mom to a career girl created another problem. The kids, more often than not, became abandoned to their own devices without parental guidance. The headlines called them "latch-key" kids! They were given a key to the house to let themselves in after school and were told to do their homework and chores until mom or dad got home from work. Fat chance on that happening! Most were busy roaming the neighborhoods and the community, making friends with other kids in the same predicament and forming gangs and establishing turf borders. Early on they might have been like the movie characters of Spanky & his gang, but eventually they became more like Butch's gang, bullying others and engaging in violence. Today they mimic their idea of "gangster" life and engage in drug trafficking, prostitution, gang violence, home invasions, robberies and drive-by shootings; so much so that it has become a national epidemic. The moral decline is reflected in how the parents lament the loss of their child when things go south for the miscreant and they blame everybody but themselves and the lifestyle their child chose. Where was the parenting and where was the parenting of the miscreants he or she ran with? There was no stern parental control or an isolating of the kids from the streets so as to protect them from corruptive influences and harm. They either joined in the gangs or got hurt or killed! Where's the protection of the parents?

That is today's trademark American culture. Not exactly something to be proud of! And now we have modern day technologies to compound the problem because those technologies don't just enhance our everyday life, they enhance the thug's life and their predatory behavior as well.

Traditions exist to maintain a culture and to refresh memories of why they exist. With the deterioration of the family structure and its influence on the community and its future through how it raised its kids, many traditions that were established for the good of the people, went by the wayside and have long been forgotten, (except for a few "old-schoolers" here and there). The husband bringing home the bacon as sole provider was one of those traditions until women entered the workforce and the economy became so bad for us commoners, that the average household needed more than pop's income to make ends meet. (Not a bad time for B & I as they got fatter at our expense!) The second income was no longer an option because of the inflating of prices.

Having to go from one income source for the average household to having to have multiple incomes just to make ends meet is not progress and is not an improvement to our economic well being, as the politicians and Corporate America want you to believe. We get to hear their rhetoric every election cycle either boasting about how great things are under them or how great they could make things if they were in power. It's all lies! There's absolutely no intent to change the socioeconomic relationship between labor and business because that would hit them in the pocket book. Instead, they just promise more jobs and the elimination of competition for those jobs which is a deception.

Everybody talks about tax reform and my response is, hogwash! It has been mathematically proven that this country could raise nearly double the revenues with just one simple tax and all the other taxes could be done away with, and the whole of the lot of them know this. One penny on the dollar could fund everything and with money left over! Why then do they insist on staying with the same tax plans that they, themselves claim are bad? Because then there would be no cadre of lobbyists greasing palms to get loopholes and they would lose control over our personal resources and assets, which they use to influence and manipulate us! With no lobby interests, who will finance their campaigns to stay in power?

Another tradition that has been compromised was women being the anchor of the household. Stay-at-home mom's job is long, arduous hours, full of stress and no financial benefits, and frankly not many can handle it, especially men. I'm amazed at how many men, especially young men, can't take care of themselves. They can't cook, they can't clean house, they don't know how to do the laundry, don't know how to mix formula or change a diaper and don't know how to handle kids. What in the world were their parents doing during their formative years? Those are all skills that are taught by the parents within the home by assigning chores, show and tell and by living the example. If the parents are absent then who is doing the teaching? The gang of kids running the neighborhood? Cultural traditions have their place in the stabilization of home and community. If you don't have the complete home in which to practice the traditions then how are the offspring going to learn them and embrace them or be in a position to pass those lessons down to their children? The 20th Century was an era of transitions and obviously, not all of them were good. In looking back over the years, humanity had a lot of traditions that went horribly wrong but there were a lot that were religiously right as well. For some reason, by the time the 60's rolled around, we were throwing the baby out with the bath water. Instead of hanging onto that which worked and throwing the bad out, we threw it all out and what we adopted in its stead is worse than all that history can cough up.

Under Old School, women were treated as possessions and frequently treated no better than one would treat a beast of burden or a family pet. That was bad. The liberation of women from this kind of behavior on the part of men was a good thing. In the 50's and before then, domestic violence was considered family business and not a violation of the law, even though it was. The spotlight was thrown on this malfeasance one day when a drunken husband beat his wife almost to death and dragged her out to the front yard and tried to finish her off with neighbors and a cop standing by and doing nothing. Finally one neighbor knocked the cop down and got into the fray and pulled the husband off of her. I can't remember for sure how it ended, but I think the perpetrator went for the cop's gun and somebody else shot him. When the story hit the papers, politics and attitudes changed but not by very much. Assault is assault, whether it happens within the confines of the home or in a bar. Domestic violence is still treated under a completely different light than violence in public with strangers. In some states, ours included, if there is evidence of domestic violence, somebody's going to jail, period; and if there's no clear aggressor, then both parties will end up going to jail where the courts can sort it out.

Child welfare and child safety has become a totally different environment. There was a time when if you acted up in school, you not only got disciplined by the teacher or principal, you caught it when you got home too. There was nothing wrong with corporal punishment and applying the board of education to the seat of understanding pretty much kept the decorum of the classroom in check. As usual, there are always those who can't control themselves and take things to the extreme, in this case, harm to a student. There was a teacher in New York who got ticked off at a student and threw a rather large dictionary, I think it was, at the student and hit her in the head causing serious injuries. A lawsuit came out of that and the curbing of schools using corporal punishment to maintain peace and order in the classroom began. Ever since then, other social malfeasances and degenerative behavior occurred that has literally outlawed any hands on control of unruly students whatsoever, even for the police. Even the cops have to use kid gloves when dealing with these little "animals" that see fit to disrupt the classroom and assault other students. Where are the parents? They're trying to find a way to make a fast buck off the school system for manhandling their precious, little, homegrown animal. They protect little Johnny or Jenny from suffering any repercussions from their malicious conduct and so they grow up figuring they can do whatever they want without getting hurt. They continue to grow up with this misconception until they finally run afoul of the law and start racking up a rap sheet or get shot and then, of course, the parents come back with, "my Johnny is such a good boy, he wouldn't harm anybody!" (Social decay!)

While I'm on the subject of "poor little Johnny", lets do this "snitches get stitches" thing the thugs have going for them. For me, a "snitch" is somebody that runs around dropping dimes on people just for the fun of it or to make trouble, like getting somebody arrested so that they can take their place on the corner selling drugs. That's snitching! Coming forward with the truth to take out the trash is not snitching. Being a good witness for a heinous murder is not snitching. That's being responsible and being of service to the community and your own family. Today's thugs have no rules. They think that fear is respect. It isn't! Fear is fear! Respect is earned, not forced! You earn it by doing right by others, not threatening them, assaulting them or murdering them. This has been a fundamental change in cultural values; a change that is not for the better and it has its roots in the lack of proper parenting and parental control.

Now, in steps "Granny Do Right", (psychiatrists and parents against corporal punishment), who made an issue over parental use of corporal punishment to control their kids and invoke discipline. They now come knocking on your door as DCF, Child Protective Services and whatever other political moniker they show up under, to bring down the full force of the law upon parents that use it. Why should it be any wonder why we have thousands of times more two legged animals desecrating our streets and communities than past generations? I'm not saying that they are 100% wrong but they are when they apply their concept blanket wide, as though all parents are child abusers, and yet that is the approach these government agencies take towards parents that make their kids tow the line and use corporal punishment to do it. Yes, we have parents that are abusers, especially those that are alcoholics or meth-heads who are prone to violence but you can't apply this concept to all parents. I can understand the agency's choice to err on the side of safety for the kids sake but then that err needs to be fully investigated, and immediately, to make sure of its legitimacy. Being pulled away from your parents can be more traumatic than the abuse, especially if there is no abuse! People who use child abuse complaints to get vengeance or to harass others should receive serious jail time and fines, with compensation to their victims. If we hear the kids wailing for some time or a baby incessantly wailing for a long period of time, or loud arguing, yes, call the cops to do a welfare check, not make an abuse complaint.

Just to make it clear, corporal punishment is not the "go-to" for disciplining a child. I used it but it was used after several warnings or when one of the kids did something that could have gotten them killed or seriously injured. I wanted to make sure they got the full message immediately and well understood, and it worked for me. Not all kids take to corporal punishment. I've got a great grand kid that it has no effect on whatsoever. At least not for his parents! He has more of an attachment to me than he does to his parents and I think its because I don't placate him; I give him genuine attention and so when I discipline him, he takes it personally and that's what makes it effective. Most of the kids got away with being given a time out but it wasn't until they were old enough to understand what was happening and feel emotional about it that corporal punishment worked. No one methodology fits all. All kids are different and they all take correction differently. You just have to find out what works and what doesn't. That is parenting! This is another skill that has suffered because parents didn't pass them on to the next generation and which has affected cultural changes that should not have been tampered with. As you can see, the parental unit has tremendous influence over what kind of people will be occupying our country in the immediate future and beyond!

This comment is going to seem a bit racial but I think it needs to be said. During the years of slavery and for a long time thereafter, blacks were deprived of a proper education, setting them back centuries, intellectually, from their captors and American society. It wasn't until President Johnson kicked open the school doors and gave them equal access that they began to have a chance at catching up with the rest of the world. Those of us who were fortunate enough to be born white, had the privilege of having educated parents that could assist in our education and that gave us a head start on the black community. This circumstance left them lagging behind the rest of America intellectually and culturally. Those that were fortunate enough to have well educated parents that were involved in their tutoring, excelled intellectually and even achieved greatness. A few others were exceptionally self motivated to achieve great things, including an education. There is a lag time involved in the intellectual history of the black community which is gradually being overcome but it is still tainted by the echoes of hatred and anger towards Whitey, that their parents and grandparents passed down to the generations that followed them. They are at a disadvantage because of these things because the resentment prevents them from wanting to stay the course and achieve as complete an education as possible. Their dropout rate is considerably greater than the white population's and it's because of the frustration that the hatred and anger fosters. It distracts them from being motivated or focused on getting educated or achieving a career or greatness, other than a life of crime, drugs and violence, (which, in their eyes is easy money). I don't take this condition as being representative of the majority of the black community but as the old saying goes, "it's the squeaky wheel that gets the grease!" In other words, its the overt activities of the miscreants that labels the entire population, just like a minority of racists get the entire white population labeled as racists by the black community. As a result, no matter what Whitey does, it tends to be labeled racist; and there are certain popular organizations that are eager to capitalize on this for personal gain and notoriety. Both sides like to play the race card as they point the fingers of blame, especially some of those in leadership positions that should know better. Democrats are exceptionally fond of playing the race card. As pointed out before, they championed slavery from day one because they wanted to exploit blacks, (reference Senator Calhoun's speech to the Senate in February of 1846).

dem·a·gogue
['demə‚gäg]

NOUN
a political leader who seeks support by appealing to popular desires and prejudices rather than by using rational argument.
synonyms: rabble-rouser · agitator · political agitator · soapbox orator · firebrand · [more]

(in ancient Greece and Rome) a leader or orator who espoused the cause of the common people.

Above is an excerpt from an online dictionary about what a demagogue is. When you start listening to all the political rhetoric, especially around election time, look at the definition of a demagogue, as cited above and see who fits the description. Pay attention to who is paying miscreants to disrupt the opposition's rallies, who is getting on their soap box and telling you to burn and loot your own community or tells you that you're just as qualified as someone with a Phd, for a particular job when you have a limited education; they're playing the race card. These are evil, divisive people who want to muddy the waters and exploit the gullible for personal gain, be it financial, political or social. As the old saying goes, "Action speaks louder than words!" Instead of listening to the rhetoric, watch the action. Look at who is actually engaging in the violations instead of who they want you to look at!

Heroes aren't born! They are people that are willing to sacrifice themselves for others, not for the glory but because a task has to be done, frequently because they are all that is left to hear the cries of the damned and respond. America is at war. It is at war with itself and its issues are being exploited to manipulate and deceive the gullible. Who are the gullible? "Low Information Voters" ring a bell? "Too stupid to comprehend, let alone vote on...." ring a bell? "Low Information voter" is just a fancy way of calling you ignorant! It wasn't the Republicans or Independents that called the public that in public and in writing and over the airwaves, it was the Democrats. They apparently are of the opinion that they are of superior intellect, compared to you, the commoner, which is in lock-step with the party's ancestry and their espoused ideology from the days of our founding when they weren't yet called Democrats. (Study the history of the Constitution and the Declaration of Independence and study the debates that took place!) Don't just jump on my bandwagon because I sound right. Get the information for yourself and go on that! Unlike party leadership, I screw up from time to time and unlike party leadership, I do my best to fix my shortcomings to comply with the truth.

The Democratic Party is cited as being the party of the working class and for the most part, it is, or was! Obviously, a "pick and shovel" mentality is inferior to the educated mentality of those who run for office, at least on paper. When the candidates go stumping around the country trying to drum up votes, they're no better than a used car salesman at making a sales pitch to us to garner our support. Superior intellect is a deciding factor, not a coronation! (Adolf Hitler was said to be an educated genius but he was anything but benevolent!) In the debates of the founders, the one group figured that their superior intellect, wealth and social status was an automatic coronation while the other side of the argument said "No", it is only a qualifier and that the people to be governed must get to decide who is the most qualified to lead. Thankfully, we went with "government by the consent of the governed"! Unfortunately, our choices haven't proved out to be all that great over the past three or four generations. The thing about the people we elect is that they represent the character and values of the people that elected them. What we have in Washington is what we put there and elected as being representative of who and what we are as a society. Using that as a ruler, I don't think we're fairing too well as a society, in that category! Again, it is my perspective that our country is in severe decline. Dr. King and LBJ led the charge against segregation and discrimination and overrode J. Edgar Hoover's racist behavior and resistance to change but that doesn't make them saints! We had two politicians that were indicted on a felony and yet the Democratic Party endorsed them. What does that say about your values?

All of our presidents have mixed results from their terms in office. None of them walked on water or parted the Red Sea with their staff. Fate allowed some of them to achieve great things, like the founding of this country and the emancipation of slaves, and space exploration or the literal defending of the world against deviant predators, (with the help of allies of course). This attests to the success of having leaders that are picked by the population instead of having self-appointed leaders that obtain their positions by force or threat of force, as in the case of dictators and monarchies. We've been exceptionally blessed to have the kind of leaders that we've had in spite of their flaws and malfeasances.

"We the People" need to remember that we are the governed and that we must decide on who will be doing the governing. Why then, do we go to the polls so flippantly and pull the lever on people based on what the rhetoric is instead of studying their character and values and making sure that we've got someone in place that will serve honorably? Could it be because we too are lacking in character and values? Red flags should be flying all over the place when you get some politician/candidate lying through their teeth or slandering and maligning their opposition to score a win. If they're that malicious with the pre-nups, then what are they going to do when they get into office? What are they going to think about you as the American voter? That means that we need to educate ourselves on just what our role is in this process and what our landmarks must be and not take the politicians at their word. Today's politicians are illusionists. They are skilled in the art of distraction to achieve their illusion. They want your attention diverted while they pull off their magic so that you can't figure out what they're really doing! This self-governance is provided for us by the Constitution and so it would be obvious to me that anybody advocating the replacement of our Constitution because it is archaic and out of touch with today's world, is up to something and that should be a red flag for us, especially when they have a history of anti-America behavior. It is the one document that guarantees our rights and guarantees our voice and so the assaults on it cannot be good. We've amended it several times to include more benefits to "we the people". The 18th Amendment, however, issued a restriction and that went over like a lead balloon and had to be rescinded for the good of the nation. As demonstrated, messing with our Constitution is not a good thing and must be approached with all due regard for the ramifications that a change will produce and we cannot allow the rhetoric of the "swamp" to make that decision for us. We each need to hit the books and educate ourselves, outside the realm of rhetoric, with an extrapolations of consequence for any amending we do to that document. To date, we've been extremely negligent in that process as individuals. We habitually follow the rhetoric and jump on bandwagons without checking out the validity of what we are hearing and tend to accept the rhetoric as "unbiased truth" and "in context". Most bandwagon melodies are lacking in truth and are out of tune! That's why all the hype!

In the beginning, each state was, in essence, its own country with its own sovereignty. None of the states were going to give up their sovereignty to a singular, all-encompassing government. They wanted to preserve their independence and their sovereign rights but they had a problem. None of them had the wherewithal to defend themselves against the European forces that claimed dominance over them, primarily England. They would have to join together and combine their forces and their resources in order to defeat their oppressors and win their independence and we could only do that as a unified force, not as individuals. The Northern half of the colonies had already formed a union but the South was the holdout because of the slavery ideology. Nothing in the founding documents could prohibit slavery if they were to join the union and so a "direct" prohibition was left out of our founding documents. They joined the union! Now you know how old Dixie came about and what led to the Civil War. The caveat that the South missed was the phrase, "all men are created equal". In their heads, blacks were not "men", they were possessions that looked and acted like people but were treated as beasts of burden, if you will. That's why they didn't make the connection about "all men are created equal". If everybody is equal then, obviously, nobody has a right to enslave or otherwise dominate over anybody else except by force of law, (as in arrest and conviction for crimes and subsequent incarceration) or consent. This is all information that we must be aware of if we are to protect ourselves from the subversive activities of insurgents, domestic and foreign. Of note, we are not doing such a hot job on handling that responsibility either!

We have a delicate balancing act to engage in. We have to figure out where we want to draw the line between what we consider seditious activity and the rights that are guaranteed us by the Constitution. We cannot preserve our rights if we allow seditious activities deprive us of them and we cannot deprive ourselves of them in an effort to prosecute seditious behavior. I believe that that's one of the reasons why the Supreme Court decided in favor of the defendant in regard to flag burning as being an act of free speech. Those that went after the flag burner erred in their charges and their prosecution. If they had arrested him for an act of sedition, which wouldn't have been all that hard to prove, then the turn out would have been markedly different. One of the gradients that defines an act of sedition against the United States is the intent to move the masses against the United States, not flippant conversation. Of course, this is just my opinion, which the 1st Amendment allows me to express! Ignored was the fact that this individual was trying to incite animosity towards our country and its government and alienate the affections of its citizens against their own country by slandering and maligning it, verbally and with the desecration of the flag, which is the definition of sedition. Because of incompetence, he got away with the defamation of the character of the United States through his actions and his rhetoric as he joined in concert with a nationwide movement of sedition against this country, which is treason. If he had a beef, (and he personally didn't, he just wanted to jump on a bandwagon and grab some of the limelight), instead of pursuing legal recourse's or getting into politics, he chose to alienate the affections of the people against their own government in support of his cause, which was pretty vague.

Here, again, where do we draw the line? We do not want to go down some slippery slope that encroaches on our "Freedom of Speech" but at some point we are going to have to draw some limitations in order to protect it. It is already understood that "Freedom of Speech" doesn't give you license to shout, "Fire" in a crowded theater unless there is really a fire and it doesn't give you a right to slander or malign someone, so we do have limitations to that freedom. If we don't allow defamation of character against the individual, then why should we allow it against our nation? If we want to prohibit the desecration of the American flag then we need to be explicit in declaring such acts as an act of sedition against this country and spell out the who, what, where, when, why and how of those conditions that make it an act of sedition. We cannot be vague about such a decree! It must fit precise parameters so that the declaration cannot be abused. If you so despise this country so much that you have no problem with defamation of character against it, then perhaps you should renounce your citizenship and find some other country more to your liking and that espouses your beliefs because it's pretty obvious that you don't consider this your country; you have no loyalty to it and are betraying it! The only thing that keeps you from being charged with treason is the fact that the charge requires the intent of mass mobilization against the country. Under the current circumstances, I don't think that it would be very hard to demonstrate that you are a part of a greater movement against this country whose ties are between organizations and movements, instead of the individual. Waiting for something grand to happen is a day late and a dollar short in regard to protecting this country against insurgency, whether it be domestic or foreign. We need some slap on the hand moments before we reach a pinnacle where people loose their lives for a fictitious cause, like the Black Lives Matter movement, which is based on a false narrative being pushed by some members of the Democratic Party out of racial bias and for personal gain.

The fact that we have a couple of generations of Americans, primarily young Americans, that engage in these Anti-American activities is an indicator that our nation is in cultural decline and that our ties to our past have been severed and the loyalty that defines patriotism has become compromised, if not brought next extinction. This is a fatal problem for this country! At this period in time we have NFL players with a national forum, that refuse to stand for the National Anthem as it is played at the start of every game. This is an act of seditious libel/treason in that it is intended to alienate the affections of the thousands or millions of people watching, against their country and for their cause, (which, by the way, is based on a false narrative). They are displaying contempt for this nation. Standing for the National Anthem is to honor this country and all that it stands for, including "Freedom of Speech". Their behavior is an act of contempt and dishonor towards all those people that contribute to the "FAT" paychecks and lavish lifestyles that this country allows them to have and the men and women that sacrificed their lives so that they can do what they do! There are other venues and means by which they can demonstrate their endorsement of their false narrative, instead of desecrating the image of America and defaming it before millions, causing themselves to look like traitors.

The cop abuse/discriminatory behavior is a false narrative that began in Ferguson, MO by liars associated with a young black person, (built like a line backer), that was guilty of strong arm robbery, assault on a police officer and the attempted murder of that police officer, (by trying to take and use the officer's gun against him). They asserted to the media that the thief had raised his hands and surrendered when nothing of the kind had occurred. He was lunging at the cop like a line backer taking out a quarter back. Other miscreant activists used this false narrative to engineer their Black Lives Matter movement and push the false narrative that cops are biased against blacks and used it to incite violence against cops and existent levels of government by preaching that cops were killing more blacks than whites in their encounters. This is flat out an act of treason, not "peaceful assembly" as protected by the Constitution. (The real score is Whitey 3 to Blacky's 1. If anybody has a right to complain, it's Whitey!) That is sedition; that is treason, because the movement is nationwide with the intent to move the masses against their country under false pretenses! Democrats were in charge during that time frame and they let everything slide. Now what does that say about their loyalty to God and Country? They won't even stand up for the country that writes their paycheck! They, (our leadership), are so detached that they don't know where the line is for where our rights become acts of sedition and treason. They are supposed to be the people's party but they are also supposed to be the guardians of our Constitution first and foremost, and they took an oath that speaks to that effect. It is the document that allows us to be participators in our own government! Without it, we become no different than a Communist regime or monarchy. We lose our voice!

On the flip side of the coin are conservative extremists that are just as far off point as the left. They are the authors of the McCarthy era that went amok and crossed the line where our rights are concerned. The intent was good, (preventing a communist insurgency), but the execution was dark! There was no restraint exercised and that, likewise, flew in the face of our Constitution and what it stands for. We do not want to go down that path again! I think their "anti-Obamacare" rhetoric fell into this category because they are the people that mocked the idea that we had a healthcare problem in this country in the first place.

Democrats are socialists, whether they carry a membership card or not, and Republicans are "capitalists", (for lack of a better description), totally fixated on making a buck. Democrats are a threat to our form of governance because they think that government, (in their minds), should be the "go-to" guy for our every need. I believe it was Karl Marx that said, "From each according to his ability, to each according to his needs", or something like that. They plow ahead without regard for the financial sustainability or viability, figuring they can always dip a little more into our pockets, especially of the wealthiest, which is what socialism is all about, diminished excesses. The Republicans believe in fiscal responsibility and if some people have to do without food or healthcare to balance the books, then so be it. I've heard some even support euthanasia as a possible solution to balancing the books. Fortunately, those individuals are not politically influential! They're just as reckless about denying social support to the community as liberals are about doling it out.

All forms of government exist for one purpose, to control the people! It is the quality of life experienced by the people, (or accepted by the people), that it governs that determines whether a government is good or bad!

Going back to economics, in the old days when we had a barter economy and even latter when we had an agronomic economy, except for a few barons, most of us were of equal socioeconomic stature because we lived off the land. We all had the same opportunities for survival and prosperity. The graphics for the socioeconomic structure of those days would have been kind of like an elongated house with a broad, low peak. Our population was distributed across the land with only a few concentrations in large cities. Today's socioeconomic graphic is that of a tall pyramid that reflects the corporate structure with only a few at the top and then a bunch more as administrators and such.

The majority of the pyramid belongs to the commoner, common labor and associates. We occupy OVER half the pyramid, the bottom half, plus! Our labors support the other two tiers of the corporate structure. We are like the statue of Atlas supporting the world on his shoulders. Because we have become an industrialized nation with an industrialized economy, our socioeconomic structure within the community and the nation is a direct reflection of the internal socioeconomic structure of business and industry. Unfortunately, the wealth is distributed the same way. The millions of peons that make up the bottom half get the floor sweepings while the other two tiers get to push away from the table with full bellies. We've gone from being dependent on nature for our survival needs, which made us equals, to being 100% dependent on the time clock and cash register for those survival needs! Our personal survival is dependent upon the mercy of Corporate America and its sharing of the wealth through their control of the time clock and the cash register.

Both of those upper tiers tend to forget that it is our blood and sweat that makes them the "fat cats!" In their efforts to squeeze blood from a turnip and maximize their profits at our expense, they not only do harm to us but they sow the seeds of bad karma that is going to come back to bite them. I just wish that it could bite them to the same degree that their behavior bites us. Unfortunately for us, they make enough money off of us to have fat bank accounts and investments to fall back on when the well runs dry because of their greed. The Democrats have the perfect solution; "come to papa, we'll bail you out," to mimic their critics! Where are we in all of this? We're still getting the floor sweepings! Both parties drink from the same well and could care less about where the water comes from. If they play us and placate us, then in their minds, the well will keep producing water and they'll keep sitting pretty!

If we were to get nuked tomorrow, (EMP), and end up back in the stone age, our socioeconomic structure would immediately return to the flat house architecture and those of us with the knowledge and experience can return to the land and the world of barter; (at least until enemy tanks come rolling in)! This is because the socioeconomic pyramid that we currently conform to would be instantly gone and the wealth that the upper two tiers enjoy will suddenly become worthless. (American money is only good if America continues to exist!) They will be instantly knocked down to our size and because of their lack of survival skills, will once again be dependent upon us, and our mercy, for their survival but this time on a personal level, not as a community. (There's a bright lining to every cloud, I guess; this one being watching their karma return to them and getting knocked down to our level.)

Business and industry must take responsibility for their role in the good and welfare of the economy and "we the people". They financially control the economy at both ends of the spectrum, unlike in the old days, and that puts them in control of our ability to survive and thrive. Market demand is subject to their control because it is they that decide what the commoner, (the majority per capita of the population), can afford to purchase, and that creates the cash flow that defines the economy that keeps all of us alive. If we can't afford what they are producing then the economy has to shut down because we can't affect the cash flow that gives life to our economy. The more people get laid off, the more market demand is diminished. All the other economic algorithms are subject to this one algorithm. All the socioeconomic math must succumb to this primary algorithm. Unfortunately for us commoners, we're caught in the middle and get it stuck to us from both ends because the "haves" consider the "have-nots" to be nothing more than whiners and complainers that can pull themselves out of their circumstance but are just too lazy to do so. How often do we have to listen to the pundits and their parrots echo that assessment? A choked economy is a figment of the imagination, as far as they're concerned; but of course when the karma comes back on them, guess who is first in line for the hand outs? If business and industry is not going to control their behavior and "share the wealth", so to speak, then "we the people", as government, are going to have to dictate the redistribution of wealth instead of the time clock, which is not good! One thousand, two thousand or even five thousand percent markups are detrimental to the good and welfare of this country and its socioeconomic well being, not to mention the damages it does to us as individuals at the cash register. Get it under control, Corporate America! In the old days, way back, the principles of tithing were applied to how much you marked up your product. It was viewed as godly and right! It was a good practice because it kept everything from being artificially inflated and unaffordable to the many. Of course this didn't apply to luxury items that people deemed that they could do without and was not a necessity for survival.

So far, I've touched on "community", "family", "church" and "economics" and how they've been compromised. Perhaps one of the most vulnerable institutions is Academia and its responsibility as the caretaker of American and world history, which is the map to our future. The topic itself is vulnerable to manipulation and corruption by those with nefarious intent or agendas. It is not enough to teach the truth! The atmosphere in which we teach and how those teachings are presented have everything to do with how it is portrayed and received. One of the lessons I learned in Drama class is that words can be spoken with dozens of different inflections so that each time it is spoken, it is received differently without changing its spelling or context. Think about how many different ways that you can say "Hi" and instill a different kind of response each time. Say it hatefully and you incite a similar response. Say it joyously and you incite a light atmosphere and generally a positive response. Groan it out and you imply that you don't feel well or are feeling down. Now apply those techniques to teaching about America and add a little spin to your dialogue. All of a sudden you are manipulating the minds of your students to view what you are teaching in a negative light and inciting ill will towards their own country. When other countries or cults practice this, it is called "brain washing". The truth gets washed out so that the false narrative can take root!

Our actions are compliant with the master law of physics called "cause and effect!" This one law applies to everything in the universe, including God! The only alternative to "cause and effect" is non-existence! Cause and Effect applies to our every day conversations and to the exchange of knowledge in the classroom and the community. The evidence suggests that America has been presented in a negative light ever since the 50's in retaliation to the McCarthy assault on Academia. I watched a newscast in the 50's where in a professor from a California university was confronted over perpetuating communism and the communist experience. His response was, "don't knock it until you try it!" It wasn't too long after that, that the 60's kicked in and communal living became the new lifestyle, along with rebellion against Corporate America, government, family traditions and the traditional family architecture, church and, of course, the Vietnam War. Overnight, our culture was turned on its head and people began to lose their lives due to our cultural wars. We lost our way as we abandoned the road maps we inherited from our predecessors and our founders. We've gone from peaceful neighborhoods and a productive America to a culture of violence, drugs, prostitution, immorality and slothfulness that has produced leaders that are reflective of the same values. That's why DC is called a swamp! Personally, I think of it as a sewer and it has a lot of nasties floating around in it.

My father taught me that when you point a finger at somebody, you need to pay attention to the other three fingers that are pointing back at yourself! Look at who is pointing the fingers and study where the other three are pointing! I'm sure you're going to start smelling something very quickly!

In the early 2000's, can't remember the exact date, a teacher was arrested and charged with treason, not because she was a spy but because she had organized her grade-schoolers into an act of insurrection. She was a product of Academia! In Texas, a teacher was fired for teaching her grade-schoolers that our founders were terrorists and that members of ISIS were "Freedom Fighters!" She was a product of Academia! In random street interviews, as students were leaving their hallowed halls of education, they were asked their opinion about America. Nine out of ten ranted against their own country and blamed their own country for all the ills of the world. Whose rhetoric were they swallowing? They didn't enter college or the university with that attitude but they sure came out of it with that attitude. This is happening in-mass, in class! This is indicative of an orchestrated sedition of the affections of the people for their country and I'm fairly sure that the malicious attitudes are divorced from their roots, which I assign to the 50's generation of

Academia that initiated the rebellion. That's the whole thing about sedition; it slithers in and silently destroys everything it touches.

Sedition is a solicitation of one's loyalties and we pretty much practice it all the time, just not against our government. When we ridicule somebody's ride and exalt our own, we are trying to solicit the affections of the other guy away from his ride and recruit him to our brand and design, are we not? That's why we show off; to solicit everybody's hoorahs!

When we boo one team and exalt ours, what do we hope to achieve? We're wanting the other guys to feel inferior and incapable of winning. In a sporting sense, we're hoping to hurt their egos and take the wind out of their sails so as to diminish their exuberance for winning and then perhaps lose because of a diminished enthusiasm for winning!

Contractors, (especially the fly-by-nighters), critique your home for its flaws in an attempt to solicit your business and make money sprucing up your house!

These are all forms of sedition! So what is it when somebody trashes your country, its integrity and its character? What are they trying to achieve? Are they trying to sell you a paint job? Trying to get you to replace your old house with the one they just happen to have in their hip pocket? Pay attention to the tune that the bandwagons are playing because they're trying to sell you on something and that, right there, warrants a red flag!

Impeachment is the same as an indictment except that it is done by the House of Representatives. The actual trial is conducted by the Senate where the determinations are evaluated and the requirements of the law are carried out. In addition to that, those same people are subject to prosecution by Federal law for their malfeasances outside the political forum.

In 2010, one of our representatives committed a felony by helping an escaped felon to be harbored outside the jurisdiction of the United States. Her malfeasance became treason when she colluded with a foreign agent/enemy to provide that sanctuary. She was called on the carpet but never prosecuted or impeached because her political party controlled both houses, the White House and the long arm of the law that is supposed to enforce our Federal Laws and have our backs. She got a pass because of political favoritism. Republicans couldn't do anything because they didn't hold the majority vote of either house. This is political corruption. This is the swamp and its creatures at work and they are fully backed by a constituency that doesn't have a problem with it because, in their heads, it's only politics.

In 2008, before Obama was sworn in and before she was seated in an official capacity, another representative went abroad and met up with a hostile foreign leader and deliberately lied to him about the intentions of the United States, Israel and Palestine to deliberately damage the White House and its peace efforts. That is blatant treason! She was called into committee to explain herself. Again, the Democrats were taking over the White House and control of both houses of Congress and so there would be no impeachment or trial and of course, no action by law enforcement which was ideologically bought and paid for by the Democratic Party. As far as her constituents are concerned, not a problem; it's only politics! This is the cesspool that our new president, Trump, has inherited and he is not politically savvy enough to deal with it. He can't just hand these little minions their paycheck and kick them to the curb. The garbage is home to roost no matter what. It's going to take at least four voting cycles to take out the garbage and I don't know of anybody that's going to help because they've all got their hands in the cookie jar in one way or the other!

The thing that gets me is that they do their malfeasances out in the broad daylight for the whole world to see and brag about it and there's nobody honest enough or of good character enough to call them out and remove them from all levels of government and governmental influence. None! That's like New Yorkers standing around and watching a woman fight for her life against a mugger and won't lift a finger to help her, not even call a cop; and this has happened on more than one occasion! And then they have the audacity to stand around and criticize their cops?

How about we consider the topic of collusion with Putin/Russia? There's a half dozen primary actors which are suspect of having been directly involved with collusion to facilitate the authorization of the Uranium-1 deal and the details of their exploits are just now coming to light. I'm suspecting a host of the loudest mouthed politicians and we can add to that list the secondary players that ran interference for them as high ranking members of our judicial system. Start digging into their relationships during the Uranium-1 deal. (Who sat on what committees and colluded with certain Federal officials and perhaps even with an enemy agent?) We are now seeing some payoffs in regard to the Iranian deal and the deal with Putin involving a private enterprise. Follow the money! At the time of this writing, it seems somebody received huge quantities of cash, which was shared to a certain extent, as an incentive to set up the uranium deal and laundered it through their not-for-profit organization. At least that's the current accusations! All the details haven't come out yet but we're getting there. Around about the same time, another representative swung a deal with another foreign agent to put a Russian owned filling station/shop-and-go, in his district. It made the headlines! They even posted a picture of him and that foreign agent toasting to its success with a coffee and a Doughnut. If you're going to live in a glass house then I would suggest you not be throwing bricks! These individuals are no longer in charge of Washington and so now the shoe is on the other foot and that means all their dirty little secrets are vulnerable to exposure. If they win back Capitol Hill, you can bet that there will be tit-for-tat repercussions, after all, it's only politics! Our national image is the least of their concerns! When are the American people going to wake up and realize that the word "politics" is not a license to throw moral turpitude in the sewer and attempt to operate above and beyond the law and abuse power, position or authority to do harm to others? When are constituents going to take their own cash cow, (a good jargon for hiring a thief to steal for you), to the barn or put it out to pasture? Ignoring the malfeasances of our politicians simply because they are our cash-cow, is going to cost us our country and make the experiment our founders entrusted to us, to fail and that means a return to the malformed type of governance that our ancestors fled from.

Reluctantly, this is why I'm in favor of term limits. We the people tend to hang on to whomever we've got and don't like to venture forth with somebody new; and so expecting the voter to enforce term limits by the vote is going to be a bit much. We get somebody we like and we don't want to see them go. When we get somebody really good, it seems some jack-wagon has to shoot them. Term limits will break the good old boy network that remains deeply seated in Congress because of tenure and our penchant for voting for the incumbent instead of somebody new. "A bird in the hand is worth two in the bush" has become our nemesis because it keeps bad apples in power and bad apples tend to contaminate all the other apples. Term limits is going to cull out the bad apples from time to time and break the cycle of spreading decay caused by tenure at the hands of the negligent voter who is afraid to roll the dice on replacing their incumbent. I don't like the idea that an excellent elective would have to be mandatorily replaced by a time limit but time has proven that getting that kind of person in place is very rare.

The other problem is that the institution of government, as soon as it is formed, takes on a life of its own and if the people who want to become a part of it don't play by its rules then they don't get to play at all! That leaves them and their constituents without a voice. Therefore, whatever party rules the Hill gets to silence the others unless they kowtow to their wishes. Democrats are notorious for this behavior and Republicans are a close second as they learn from their nemesis's. Term limits will break this pattern of self-destruction that they all are caught up in.

There is a serious disadvantage to having term limits. Much of the rest of the world, especially enemy nations, do not have term limits. Their leadership stays in place for generations and that gives them an edge on us because their individual leader can attain years of experience and learning on us and develop ties that provide an information network and external support towards achieving their agendas that we can't develop.

To counter this deficiency, we would have to develop a superior covert information network that can keep Capitol Hill up to speed on what is going on behind closed doors around the world. How business gets done on Capitol Hill will probably have to be revised since there won't be generational ties connecting party agendas from one legislative movement to another. (Currently, we can table legislation or bits of legislation, or pigeon hole them, until such time as conditions become more favorable for following their agenda. If the old guard is gone then so are the ties and the agenda and the legislation becomes subject to new eyes. A process for dusting off the shelves from time to time will probably have to be pursued.)

I think we could work around that difficulty if we go to term limits, which would be the lesser of two evils.

CHAPTER VI

The Flip Side

Everything in life has a flip side and all blessings carry a curse. "Cause and Effect!"

In the years prior to the 20th Century, we lived off the land. We prospered according to our own right and was not controlled by the mechanics of social reform. We were only controlled by the forces of nature and matters of conscience. Your neighbors were miles away unless you lived in a settlement and even then you had plenty of elbow room to do your thing without being a nuisance to everybody else. A settlement could only grow so large and then you began to have a problem with the accumulation of human and animal waste and the odors that came with it. If you need some graphics, just imagine everybody in town having a couple of horses for a buggy and one for a saddle and the excrement that they would produce. What are you going to do with all that waste and its stench for a city of say 100,000 people? Now imagine trying to provide sewage for a condo or hotel with today's population and the lack of amenities likened the past! Where would all that waste go? Providing accommodation for these accumulating problems was slow in coming and so diseases, like the plague, hit metropolitan areas like Paris and New York and many other densely populated areas of the world and the nation. That was quite a downside to living in a densely populated area that provided amenities that you had to provide for yourself if you lived in the remote expanses of early America. The downside to living in remote areas was that if you got fatally sick or injured, you were toast! Doc Holiday wasn't just around the corner! If you were having a problem with cattle rustlers, bandits or thieves, you had to take the law into your own hands because the nearest law enforcement might be a hundred miles or more away, a three or four day trip on horseback, if the bad guys didn't get to you before you got to the law. Many of the pioneers that gave up the country life for city life, brought this do-it-yourself concept with them and that, taking the law into your own hands, posed a problem. Having vigilante posse going after the wrong guy because of false assumptions and without a trial to determine guilt or innocence made for a serious problem.

The upside to all of this was a society that minded their P's & Q's and respected each other's ability to react to a threat. Kind of an antique version of "mutual self-destruction", which was the theme of the nuclear arms race.

The 19th and 20th centuries were an explosion of technological advancements in communications, transportation and domestic conveniences. The advancements in domestic conveniences catered to our laziness and the desire to do more with less, with its impact concentrated in areas of dense population where their characteristics could be exploited to the max. It allowed us to do more with less bodily energy and commitment and so a trend towards obesity from the lack of exercise became apparent. About midway the twentieth century, maybe a little later, schools began cutting out recesses as it was viewed as a waste of time; time that could be used for the studies needed to keep us intellectually ahead of our international competitors and could perhaps get the teachers off work a bit sooner through shortened class time. As the result of the elimination of this aerobic activity, obesity began to set in and intellectual performance began to decline.

The theory behind the decrease in intellectual performance was that it was due to the lack of aerobic exercise. The brain requires oxygen in order to perform like it should and the oxygenation of the brain requires peak blood flow. The lack of aerobic exercise slows down the circulatory system thereby reducing oxygen distribution and consumption to all the body's organs, especially the brain and so a deficiency of achievement began to become apparent all across the student spectrum. We are now into the 21st century and obesity awareness is front and center but many of the schools still haven't re-instituted active recess programs stressing aerobic activities to burn off calories, to burn off the pounds and oxygenate the system, especially the brain. I'm guessing that we are going to have to use some ingenuity to accomplish this feat because many of those who are now obese are probably very self-conscious about their condition and don't want to make a public spectacle of themselves as they struggle against their condition. A little discretion should be in order.

Of recent discovery was the impact that marijuana and gaming electronics have on intellectual acuity.

I got this from off of wiki the other night and I think it bears taking under consideration.

Clinical significance[edit]

This section needs expansion. You can help by adding to it. (January 2017)

High alcohol consumption has been correlated with significant reductions in grey matter volume.[5][6] Short-term cannabis use (30 days) is not correlated with changes in white or grey matter.[7] However, several cross-sectional studies have shown that repeated long-term cannabis use is associated with smaller grey matter volumes in the hippocampus, amygdala, medial temporal cortex, and prefrontal cortex, with increased grey matter volume in the cerebellum.[8][9][10] Long-term cannabis use also alters white matter integrity in an age-dependent manner,[11] with heavy cannabis use during adolescence and early adulthood causing the greatest amount of damage.[12]

Meditation has been shown to change grey matter structure.[13][14][15][16][17]

Habitual playing of action video games has been reported to promote a reduction in grey matter.[18][19]

I came across this information while studying nervous system structure and its mechanisms and found it to be fairly interesting. We are all aware, (well, except for on the part of the alcoholics perhaps), of the damage that alcohol has on the brain and liver but I wasn't too clear on the impact of cannabis on the brain. I wonder what the trade off is between losing grey matter at the hippocampus, amygdala, medial temporal cortex, prefrontal cortex and the increase in the cerebellum is going to be!

The other two things that got my attention was the fact that "meditation" changed grey matter structure. In brain studies, it was found that people like Einstein had more folds in their grey matter than other people. This tells me that the more folds the brain has, the more efficient you become at thinking and that serious meditation can improve those conditions.

The other part of the study that surprised me was that all those electronic games that we enjoy so much and engulf our kids with seems to diminish grey matter, (that's the part of the nervous system that processes information and tells the rest of the body what to do through the connections of the white matter/nerves, (putting it simply).

Apparently, our electronic gadgetry is killing us intellectually! I think that qualifies as a bad flip side to our happy top side to electronics. As I've said, every blessing carries with it a curse. Abusing or taking for granted the blessing activates the curse. We Americans tend to always take things to the excess! We are never happy with "moderation"! We even take our laziness to the extreme!

Improvements in communications and transportation were a contributing factor to our nation becoming an alcoholic nation and the 18th Amendment and the crime spree that followed, by making the manufacture and distribution of alcohol efficient. We are always ready to take advantage of availability! We most likely wouldn't have the drug problem we have today if we didn't have all the means of distribution and communications that we so easily take advantage of today in our personal lives. Those two attributes have been like plant food to our penchant for addictions!

Where is our government in all of this? We the People are the government, remember? It was "We the People" that passed the 18th Amendment and thoroughly screwed things up, remember? It was "We the People" that took over all wilderness, (unoccupied), lands so that nobody could just go out and stake out a claim for themselves without some real estate broker or government agency picking their pockets dry and thereby took away our ability to live off grid and free from the financial predators of government and society.

With today's knowledge, we could have allowed people to live off grid in designated, protected areas, like the national parks, so long as they conformed to the demands of nature, and use them to help monitor and even police the wilderness to the benefit of the wilderness areas and towards a reduction in costs experienced by government policing activities. Teaching such people how to do wildlife assessments and counts, basic wildlife management techniques and animal husbandry would be a tremendous asset towards the preservation of our national and state parks. Tenants living off the lands would be able to help keep dead wood from accumulating and becoming a fire hazard around where they live as they use it for heating and cooking and could be used to target game excesses by culling the excessive abundance of some wildlife that gets out of balance with the ecosystem. The big thing is, they get to live off grid and unannoyed by government controlled lifestyles and civilization and we get to reap the benefits. They would just have to realize that they are a part of the wilderness scene and wilderness experience for adventurers and can't expect not to have visitors on their turf and would be expected to act like a park ranger and not a hostile land owner if a tourist should wander through! The whole idea behind national and state parks is to preserve the wilderness conditions and natural wonders and having natural guardians in them would enhance that purpose. Just a thought!

CHAPTER VII

After thoughts -

Political strategies:

One of the tactics used in crime and warfare is the art of distraction and diversion in order to achieve a goal or agenda. You create an explosion to draw everybody to the site so that you can rob a bank far away from the site so that there's nobody left to pursue you. You distract and divert the enemy's attention to facilitate your landing from another direction as the United States and Britain did to Hitler to facilitate the D-Day landings. Politicians are especially adept at doing this. I figured this out when the Republicans resisted JFK's candidacy. They muddy the waters and stir up accusations against an opponent with the right hand so that you don't notice what they're doing with their left! Where there's smoke, there's fire, except that the fire isn't always where the smoke is! Sometimes when you're trying to escape the smoke, you run into the fire! It's far better to be away from it all so that you can get a bigger view of what's going on! As any forest fire fighter will tell you, you need eyes in the air, not just on the ground, so that you can get a true picture.

When Trump was running for the presidency, the political left was busy muddying the waters with accusations of sexual misconduct and collusion with enemy states. This past month, (October/November

2017), it seems that his accusers are being found guilty, (in the court of public opinion), of those very things, and worse. Smoke and mirrors!

They made accusations of collusion with Russian agents to engage in political and personal business! Guess what? It turns out his accusers were not only colluding with Russian agents but were accepting bribes from them and using their private charities to launder the money. Smoke and mirrors! (What gets me is even with the disclosures, their parrots continue to worship at their feet.)

A typical election tactic is to go out in a fake "get out the vote" campaign and promise people a ride to the poles. The fake is that they promise rides to both sides of the isle but only pick up those voting on their side, and then they dare blow smoke up everybody's derriere about somebody skewing the election!

ACORN was a political activism organization brought about by the coordinated efforts of the labor unions and the Democratic Party which organized them off the books and under the radar so that there would be no paper trail or money ties to them. They organized them to be a completely separate, self-sustaining entity. We were instructed to go out and find member activists that wanted to get engaged but didn't have a position within our organization and show them how to organize, set up the non-profit and how to generate revenues. Their focus would be on low to moderate income earners and they would help organize community groups, like neighborhood associations, crime watch, etc., but one of the chief reasons for setting up the organization was to generate a voting block loyal to the Democratic Party by using the people's issues to generate support; "never let a good catastrophe go to waste!" They got hammered when they got caught in their slight-of-hand tactics and advisories to their targets. The good and welfare of the people was not their target, the achieving of political agendas was. Smoke and mirrors! ACORN stands for the Association of Community Organizations for Reform Now.

On the surface, the organization sounds and looks legit, but it was the little foxes that destroyed the vine!

Never underestimate the loyalty to ideologies. In the 2016 cases against the directors of the IRS and the EPA, Obama did not give them orders to pursue the anti-conservative agendas that they pursued. They pursued their strategies because of their loyalties to Obama and the Democratic Party, not right or wrong, and shared ideologies with the leadership of the Democratic Party. They figured the boss would be pleased with how they handled themselves! Little Nixonites! Again, the ideology of, "if it's political then it's OK!" For some reason, there's a philosophy out there that says that if something is political then you have license to flush your honor, integrity and credibility down the toilet so you can pursue your agenda, even if it's dead wrong! They then roll the dice and if they win then they figure all's justified; "the end justifies the means!" (Another cliché that lends justification to throwing your honor, integrity and credibility in the garbage!)

What would you think about a person that runs for office on the premise of obtaining a piece of government owned vacant property for the purpose of creating affordable housing? While she's campaigning, she and family members buy up property all around that area. Win or loose, if that piece of property, (which she has started a reformation movement on), experiences an increase in value, then so do all the properties surrounding that area which automatically brings in a profit on those properties, flipped or not, improved or not! The agenda wasn't the improvement of the neighborhood/district; it was the pursuit of easy money! She turned the property into a nice park to accommodate the properties around the area and that drove up their values; "affordability" was not a byproduct of hers or her relatives property improvements, if any were made. Her promises were apparently empty promises with no intent of fulfilling the expectations of her constituency. The campaign was all smoke and mirrors! Not mentioning names but if you know the story then you know who I'm talking about!

Money laundering is how you separate yourself from the money trail of improper financial dealings or flat out thievery. One method involves taking a loss from your ill gotten gain. You're still making money but end up having to share a significant portion of it to get it laundered. One way is to purchase articles, a little here and a little there and then re-selling it at a reduced price. Another is to hire somebody to do pretty much the same thing, perhaps with stocks and bonds or other investments. Another method, as currently disclosed, is to have somebody, (a large organization or other entity), make a large donation to one of your organizations and then reciprocate the good deed by doing something for them for a similar fee, to be paid to you! Your organization benefits, (which just might pay you a stipend for managing), and you benefit; perfectly legal in appearance. If you are an agent of the United States government and there is a reciprocation on your part for their part, then that is not only money laundering, it is collusion with that agent. Sounding familiar?

Missile Guidance System Technology is Top Secret Classified information that we absolutely do not want enemy states to get their hands on. In 1994, or thereabouts, a certain individual, (to help an enemy state participate in space technologies), declassified our Missile Guidance System Technology and facilitated its sale to the Chinese. China is allied to North Korea and guess who is making explicit use of a very much improved guidance system technology today? This is what happens when you do not extrapolate the consequences to your actions for all possibilities and probabilities, especially where National Security is concerned! These actions were undertaken by the same guy that issued a Presidential Order to fire all "cattle guards" in the nation, no exceptions! He wanted to take the action to beat the crap out of GOP supporters! Abuse of power and authority! Look up what a cattle guard is and you'll get a good definition of "stupid is as stupid does!" Capitol Hill, especially his own party, should have taken a hint about this man's competency where the good and welfare of the nation is concerned and should have been much more vigilant! Now they've got themselves painted into a corner as the result of supporting more than one malefactor that has damaged this nation's safety and security.

The hallmark of the Democratic Party is the art of playing Robin Hood, robbing the rich and giving to the poor, (redistribution of wealth); nice concept if it were right and righteous! There's two problems with that ideology; what happens when you've stolen all the wealth and there's no more to be had? What happens to the poor that were dependent on your thievery and you can no longer deliver? The examples of that are evidenced throughout history as "third world countries" soaked in poverty and famine. The second consequence is what happens when the rich pick up their marbles and go someplace else to play! Where's your financial base then? We lost jobs, wages, benefits and tax revenues because of this negative migration from our economy while the same proponents of the Robin Hood philosophy opened the flood gates to an incoming immigration of the poor and destitute, unskilled and uneducated who must rely on the Robin Hood resources to finance their upkeep. If it were possible to take in the equivalent of the American population each year, we still would not be able to take in the proliferation of indigent peoples from around the world in an attempt to solve the world's problems of poverty and famine. It is an impossibility! Fixing their situations at home is the obvious solution, not drowning us and pulling us down financially and socially to their level where we can do nothing for anybody, just like them. We cannot dummy down our quality of life to level the playing field! We must elevate their quality of life to do it and we must do it where they live, not at our expense on our soil. Most people love where they were born and raised and would have no problem staying there if their quality of life, (their freedoms), were brought up to our standards.

"Give us your tired, your weak, your hungry" is BS! We don't have the room or the resources to do that for the whole world. What needs to be done is for their oppressors to quit creating the tired, the weak and the hungry so that we feel sorry for them! Has anybody thought about inspiring the reformation of oppressive governments and helping them to achieve our level of prosperity and peace? Why do we have traitors amongst us that would rather tear us down to a level of impoverishment equal to the rest of the world instead of elevating the rest of the world to our level of abundance?

We have college and university students running their pig pen mouths about how bad America is and about how we need to stay out of other nation's affairs and then they turn right around and demand we do something about those same people's oppressions and conditions, even to the point of taking them in, much to our own detriment. They just like to parrot their mentors, be they political or academic, that way they don't have to bother doing any learning or thinking about the problem. Again, it's the left hand using the right hand to hide what its doing and the students are unwitting accomplices to a hidden agenda. They're the smoke, their rage is the smoke! So where's the fire? Academia? The DNC? Liberalism in general? Maybe it's the "perfect storm" combination of all of them!

When the hallmarks of criminal behavior become the hallmarks of our political party then we have some serious problems. The hallmarks of the Democratic Party have been towards social malfeasances and the hallmarks of the Republican Party have been financial malfeasances. The later is dangerous to our financial well being but the former is dangerous to our very existence. Financial malfeasances we can deal with but the social malfeasances cover a broad spectrum based on ideologies which shape our cultures and our politics and those are the cornerstones of our existence. We are in mortal peril as the result of accepting lying and cheating as being honorable behavior and using "politics" as an endorsement for that kind of conduct and character. This is a cancer and it is consuming us!

Principles are the do's and do-nots of life that we apply to ourselves on a personal level. A person of principle is a person that can be depended upon to act a certain way based on his or her values. They're kind of a flexible, self-imposed Ten Commandments, since you are the author of your own principles. We want our principles to instill other people's trust in us, establish personal boundaries that we will not cross because we find doing so to be offensive to our senses. They are at the heart of honor and dignity and when we violate them we are in danger of dishonoring our own person. A person of low principles is a dishonorable person that cannot be trusted. We develop our principles over a life time from the things we were taught by our parents, by lessons learned as we integrated into society and from lessons learned through interactions with others. You build on your principles just like you work on your credit and character. It is an intentional effort to be righteous in deed and thought as we interact with the world around us! We have a class of people living amongst us that have no intention of pursuing righteousness and have no problem pointing out the faults of others to justify their own lack of morals. "Well Jimmy did it!"

Unprincipled people are prone to lying, cheating, thievery and other sordid manners of conduct, including murder. They can be counted on being deceptive in their dealings and of low moral character and conduct. They cannot be trusted in any way, except to serve themselves and violate the trust of others. Bargaining with such people is a frivolous effort on our part. Considering such a flawed character, why then do such people have loyal followings that tend to go along with anything they say? Where are those people's principles? Birds of a feather flock together? I would surmise that such persons do not like the idea of having to admit that their judgment is flawed and so they continue to try to fit the square block in the round hole.

If we are lucky enough to have principled parents, they will pass onto us their principles, like how to respect others, table manners, or even the value of religion (in moderation) in their lives. Their teachings should help you get off to a good start in life!

Rich people tend to produce rich offspring because their kids are raised under the influence of the principles that produce wealth. Poor people tend to stay locked in poverty because the principles of the rich is not one of their fortes and so there is nothing to pass down. They don't have those principles to practice or pass down to the next generation; you can't pass on what you never had, and so generation after generation stays locked into the impoverishment life cycle. On the other hand, the poor tend to base their principles on soul while the rich can be heartless and of no spiritual principles. That's why Christ said it was harder for one of them to make it into the Kingdom of Heaven than for a camel to get through the eye of a needle.

The "eye of the needle" was a low, narrow passage way that allowed foot access through the ramparts of a city or castle. It forced you into a stooped position as a defensive measure. If you were a bad guy trying to gain access, you were in the perfect position to get your head lobbed off when you poked it through on the other side. The narrowness of the tunnel prohibited you from being able to draw your sword or swing it and so you were at considerable disadvantage when you poked through! Imagine being in that space with an archer facing you at the opening!

There is a natural order to everything, based on the law of "Cause and Effect" and when man acts in concert with others, the world responds in concert, just like two people interacting on the street without the law to back one or the other up. Most of the people of the world are naturally compassionate towards one another. The dispassionate ones are generally the rich and powerful, the leadership of each country or group. They are the people that start wars and dissent and often time lie to their own to get the support they need to progress in their agenda. Remember that when you're picking sides!

Those that force their people into impoverishment so that they can live a more lavish lifestyle off the blood and sweat of the destitute are of the worse kind. They inspire movements of compassion in other countries but nobody wants to go to war to fix the problem. Their compassion is cut short by, "their problems are none of our business!" So principled! The compassionate vie to do nothing and so allow evil to do what it wants. "We cannot be the world's police force!" Remember that cliché? It's repeatedly echoed generation after generation. It was echoed prior to both world wars and so we, and others, sat back and did nothing and allowed the evils of other countries to fester and multiply until it attacked us and involved us in its war. The evils of the world forced our hand and even then we had our domestic detractors who would rather we be overrun and destroyed than go to war. That is passivism taken to the extreme, even psychotic! The conscientious objector is a person that would rather die from a bullet than use a bullet. I can respect where they're coming from but it doesn't mean that I agree because they're not sacrificing their life for another, which is what the Bible honors, and the Bible makes a distinct difference between killing and murder. It gives us an exception!

Because of unity, nations move against nations and nations move with nations to affect the evolution of man and the character of the human species. Many of today's conveniences come from military needs and technology, right down to the potato peeler. (It was a GI that designed and invented the potato peeler because he was constantly on KP, peeling potatoes. At least that's the story that I got!) Because we are a social animal, we tend to move together as a group and we develop trends. This is what happened when our nation fell off the wagon and became a nation of alcoholics which inspired the creation of the 18th Amendment. People of those days, and prior to that, drank alcohol instead of water because the alcohol didn't carry deadly diseases and parasites or go rank over time and so it wasn't that hard for millions of Americans to fall off the wagon together. ("In all things, do so in moderation," seemed to have been forgotten!) The point is that we moved as a group, by the masses. What was the inspiration? We are experiencing the same sort of mass movement within our cultural standards as our nation declines and our standards degenerate. Just like before WWI and WWII, we the people, have been taking a "stay out of their affairs" approach to the evils around the world and just like before, that "stay out of it" approach has allowed those evils to fester and grow until it now attacks our friends and us on a personal level, and just like before, we have the detractors that want to do nothing. They'd rather sell out this nation than get involved in defending the country they owe their lives too.

CHAPTER VIII

Extrapolation of Consequences

As individuals, hanging onto the past is not necessarily a good way to move ahead but as a nation, the past provides a road map to the future. By comparing where we are to where we've been, we can get a pretty good indicator as to where we are headed. In our case, we are in social decline! The recent revelations of the abundance of malfeasances being revealed about our nation's leaders from the local level to Capitol Hill is a sordid indicator of how previous generations have failed to perpetuate moral turpitude, honor and integrity in subsequent generations so that we could find honorable people to hold this nation's top positions and set examples for us to follow.

Never before in our history have we had such a malady of civil violence and criminal conduct and that points directly to a disconnect between the cultures of our past when it was safe to sit out on your porch and enjoy the peace and today when you could get shot just stepping to the door. That vets the observation that we are in serious social decline as a civilization as the result of a breakdown in family values and a lack of the perpetuation of values, virtues and traditions that once kept our communities stable and peaceful. I'm not talking about five or ten years ago; I'm talking about three or four generations back when the importance of the role that family played in our quality of life and civil order started to become ignored as the composition of our labor force, family structure and influence and American culture began to transition into an industrialized society and economy. The 50's generation lit the fuse but the 60's generation was the explosion that rebelled against all the social standards of the day. The big cities have had gangs of one kind or another throughout the 1900's but never to the extent that they have them today or during the last two or three decades of the 1900's. Again, this is evidence of social decline, not progress. Seeing a decline in the moral quality of our politicians? It is related! If you want better politicians then they have to start being raised now into the kind of person we want to see them to be when they take their place in our world!

If we're in decline then our nation is dying! The obvious question then is, how do we turn things around? The answer is quite obvious also, quit doing what we're doing! When you find yourself in a hole that's too deep to climb out of, quit digging! Unfortunately, we can't just snap our fingers and go back to where we were doing things right and start over again. We have to work our way back and that isn't going to be any kind of picnic. We have to restore our foundation and cornerstones to their original condition from before things started to go south on us. That means restoring the traditional family structure of two parents and offspring and the standards by which they raise their kids and shape their character and behavior. It means putting a stop to the anti-Christ movement in this country that is stymieing the influence of the church on the character of family and community. (The church is the repository for community standards and is responsible for perpetuating those standards through its outreach to the members. It is the only institution so dedicated!) The restoration of community is going to require strong economic changes that allows families to function properly in their roles as parents and participants in community affairs, like the PTA and community volunteer programs, like Crime Watch and Community Policing.

Today's families, (the Commoners), have to work multiple jobs to make ends meet and that deprives the parents of quality parenting time with their kids as a couple. (This is Corporate America's fault!) This is one of the necessities for having an influence on how the character of a child and his or her behavior develops. This is where the character, values and behavior of the next generation of adults and leaders is shaped. Considering our current state of affairs, I would say that this should be an "on the front burner" priority!

Over the decades we've become a loose and lascivious society with very few restrictions on social behavior. (Being in a permanently, committed relationship before producing kids, being one example!) This has created a situation where opposite genders don't dare interact with each other without the chance of it being called sexual harassment by somebody wanting to steal the limelight or hustle somebody, especially for politically motivated reasons in today's politically charged climate. People are vulnerable because of values and principles that are no longer being instilled in succeeding generations because the people that were responsible for raising this generation or the generation before that didn't want to restrict their own personal conduct. Men, especially, have always had a problem with keeping their hands to themselves and respecting the woman's space and dignity. This is especially true within the confines of the corporate office and with public figures that succumb to taking advantage of their popularity and it was especially true as women became more integrated into America's workforce. Proper upbringing means you keep your hands to yourself! It means you respect each other's space and integrity! Furthermore, it is the parent's responsibility to instill those values in their children and obviously, the importance of doing that has been lost over the past four or five generations and therefore neglected. Today, we are harvesting what our grandparents and great grandparents have sown; loose and lascivious conduct with no moral restraint!

This lack of respect for boundaries and conduct is chief among causes for teenage pregnancies and improper conduct between adults and teens; which has been commanding the headlines for over a generation now. Instead of fixing the cause of this malady and thereby employ prevention, society has chosen to increase the penalties for engaging in the behavior which is employed after the fact. God forbid that they should have to instill proper etiquette and behavior in their children and set the example!

This change cannot happen without society wide participation and society wide participation has to begin with the individual family taking responsibility for the values that get instilled in their children. We can't go back four generations and fill in the deletions of our predecessors; their failure to instill good moral social values in their children. The deletion didn't just occur yesterday, it occurred generations ago and the heirs of those consequences cannot pass down moral values that were never instilled in them and that makes it ten times as hard to turn this behavior around because the perpetrators were never taught just how wrong such conduct is.

This behavior pattern has created an environment where both genders are trigger happy. Women have reached a point where it doesn't matter what the guy does, it's going to be interpreted as either sexual misconduct or gender discrimination. Men, (responsible men), have reached a point where having anything to do with women is like trying to pick a rose without get stuck by its thorns. We tend to keep them at arm's length as a matter of self preservation and if you don't, you risk getting labeled a predator! And then you have women of this same mentality working in social agencies that view everybody as perverts until proven otherwise and have no problem putting words in children's mouths that discolor their relationship with their parents. As a result of this, and some have been caught doing it by people that could afford the legal eagles to defend themselves, kids are learning how to manipulate the system to "get even" with their parents for restrictions or punishments laid on them for their misconduct. Every thing we do, or neglect to do, has a consequence and has a ripple effect, like a person elbowing their way through a packed crowd.

As you can see from the scenario above, the thought process has very fluid dynamics within the dynamics of society. It's like that stunt we used to pull where you start a rumor at one end of the classroom to see how it got distorted by the time it reaches the other end of the classroom. Sometimes the ending story is not even close to the original story. The same thing happens because of the actions of the few that start something and as it passes around the classroom of society, it takes on a life of its own that impacts other aspects of our lives that were never the intended target. The things that the family do as they raise their kids has an expanding impact on the world around them and like the story in the school example, they make ripples throughout our social culture which are either positive or negative. Neglecting to instill morals and principles allows them to live their lives on what they determine on their own to be right or wrong. If you set back and observe society you're probably going to notice that all humans have a penchant for evil and if you look closer, you'll notice that proper behavior is a learned behavior, not natural behavior. Our natural state is that of an animal! It is when we revert to our animal instincts and behavior that we run afoul of the law and society and end up getting caged like an animal. Our number one primal instinct is fight or flight! Our number one natural edict is survival and procreation of the species. Fight or flight serves as a survival tool. Part of survival is foraging for food, seeking secure surroundings out of the elements and free of other predators. The thievery, drug dealing and other maladies of our society are all conforming to the animal survival instinct. If you're a hunter or a fisherman, you look for the most efficient way to put the food on the table. The animals of the wild don't hunt animals that can eat them, they hunt for the easy pickings that take the least effort, (conservation of energy). You ask any drug dealer why they're doing what they do and they'll flat out tell you, "easy pickens!" You ask hookers why they do what they do and they'll tell you, "easy pickens!" The consequences aren't so easy but the goal is! Thieves rob because, as far as they're concerned, it looks like easy pickens! Like most predatory animals, they look for the easy pickens or take whatever they can catch with the least effort. That is animal behavior! Living right comes from social order. Community values, (acceptable forms of conduct), are learned behaviors taught by parental observation and tutoring first and then through community interactions on a trial and error basis. I suspect that most kids engage in some level of shoplifting, even it is just one time; the game changer is their getting caught and having to face the consequences for what they have done. If they get caught right out of the starting gate, they respond pretty well to just getting embarrassed and perhaps a slap on the wrist. The more they get away with it, the more hardened they become and dignity takes a back seat. Embarrassment no longer works and some pain and suffering is needed to make the point; perhaps corporal punishment and/or deprivation of things like television, the computer, games or restrictions of some sort! After that, their activities begin to include the cops and they start to establish a pattern of malfeasances that usually expand beyond just minor thievery events. Unchecked, their animal behavior does nothing but get worse and the more convinced they become that they can get away with anything. When they get too big for the parents to control then there is no turning back. The time to exercise control and discipline is when they are toddlers and they still have that parent/child bond that excepts parental direction.

Now if the parents were raised without parental direction then the probability that they didn't exercise any control over their kids, beyond stopping them from being an annoyance, is pretty much guaranteed. People keep all kinds of dangerous animals as pets. The animals act friendly and put up with the cuddling that is generally dolled out to a pet but it doesn't delineate the fact that they are wild animals and have all the abilities necessary to kill you. Just because your wayward offspring is all snuggley at home, doesn't mean that he isn't an animal at heart, not a pussycat. It's sad to see a parent weep over the loss of a son or daughter due to their karma catching up with them but it also demonstrates how blind we can be to the malfeasances that some of our offspring engage in, even in death. Most of us love our kids and it causes us to be a lot more lenient towards them than we would be towards a stranger's kid, or even a neighbor's. Perhaps, if we loved them so much, we'd keep them attached at the hip and not allow them to associate with all the bad seed we have roaming our streets. Kind of like over protective hens! I know that at some point in time our little chicks have to venture out beyond the nest. The best we can hope for is that we've instilled in them strong enough values to withstand the evils and temptations that are waiting for them beyond the front door.

The Bible doesn't give you directions on how to raise your kid other than the fact that it is up to you to raise them into the kind of person you want them to be; a person of good character and proper behavior, I would hope! The next step would be to decide on what you want your son or daughter to be when they grow up; liars and thieves/drug dealers and pimps or the working class or better still, some sort of professional or executive? It's up to you, as a parent to lay the bricks that make up the path that you want them to follow! If you're not involved in paving the way then they're going to follow somebody else's path and then all bets are off! The lucky one's will pick up on an icon that sets an appropriate example, the others get their lessons in life from off the streets which is not an epitome of virtue. The social environment of today's communities have become too dangerous to allow youngsters free reign to roam the community without a chaperon of some kind to protect them from gang solicitations and gang violence. Being nearby also gives you a chance to intervene when they start to engage in some sort of malfeasance, like picking a fight or slight-of-hand.

Confrontation is not a natural interaction between two people. Adrenalin increases, anticipation increases and the fight or flight emotions start to get excited. Resistance to face to face confrontations is a natural state of mind. As our kids get older and older, unless there is an established pattern of authority, direction is received as confrontation and eventually things get out of control. Control over the young one becomes non existent. I've seen parents absolutely petrified at the thought of having a confrontation with their kid about their behavior and/or their intentions because of their child's potential for violence and the mature size of their kid, (teenager), and/or the possibility of having a weapon of some kind nearby. Control over these situations isn't going to happen after the fact; it has to be addressed from day one in how you bond with your child and how you interact with them and groom their loyalties and behavior. You need to be their role model, especially since the majority of their formative years are going to be with you and not the bad seed down the street.

In the old days, most of us lived off the land to one degree or another and so having chores and responsibilities to handle was a common practice. This gave us a fairly structured lifestyle that taught us how to be responsible for ourselves and those things entrusted to our care. You don't get those virtues from a textbook. They are hands on experiences which instill self-discipline towards taking responsibility for your actions and people's trust in you! This process wasn't some kind of textbook program that parents followed for programming their kids. It was just the natural results of doing what was necessary to survive off of nature and pretty much off grid in most of the country.

We've become a nation of city-slickers and no longer compete with nature for our survival; instead we are relegated to competing with business and industry for our survival and children are prohibited there! On top of that, we've become a nation of snowflakes that want to put kids in a rubber room so that they can't get hurt playing, working or doing chores, (which are the keys to instilling a work ethic, values and due consideration for others). A kid can't even open a lemonade stand without some jerk coming around and demanding they have a business license to operate their lawn chair lemonade stand and pass a health inspection and get health permits. Absolutely asinine! Kids used to be able to grab the lawn mower and mow theirs and their neighbor's lawns to earn a few bucks here and there but that was deemed much to dangerous for kids to do and so they're outlawed from mowing lawns on the thesis that they pose a threat to the marketplace of the professionals that mow lawns for a living. Why is it any wonder that they've reverted to drug trafficking and prostitution as a means to earning money? What are they supposed to do; sit around an pout because they have nothing to do and no money to do it? This is why we've seen a degeneration of the American culture to one of drugs and violence and the change has occurred over generations, not overnight! Turning away from the lucrative temptations of drugs and pimping is going to be an uphill battle, even if they were given adult privileges to engage in legitimate business pursuits. There's no way for a few dollars an hour can compete with the hundreds or thousands of dollars an hour drug trafficking can bring in and the violence engaged in to keep that kind of cash flowing is something to be expected.

Again, changing this culture is going to require isolating the new generation from those already involved, thereby keeping the new generation from the lucrative temptations and influence of the nefarious lifestyles that now define the American culture. That could be an impossible task if members of the family are using or wheeling and dealing in drugs! Street gang members need to be isolated to their homes, not just their neighborhoods, to prevent collusion and gang violence. Their assemblage is not "peaceful assembly" as protected by the Constitution. Their violence is colluded acts of insurrection against this country because they knowingly engage in activities that they know are a clear and present danger to this country and their communities, whether that was their intent or not! It's one thing to mess up and do harm "unintentionally", (wanton negligence), and quite another when you set about to keep repetitively doing the harm for personal gain and acting against the good and welfare of the state and the community. There is case precedent for this. Labor union officers are accountable for the acts of their membership whether they give the orders or not! If we, (union members), do harm to the community then not only are the members held accountable but so are the officers whether they were active participants or not. Their only exoneration is if they attempted to stop the problem and notified the proper authorities to aid in prevention.

If you want an adult that isn't foul mouthed then you raise them out of the presence of that kind of language which means you don't use it in your home, in their presence; and if they come up with that kind of language out of the clear blue, you immediately correct them and find out or figure out where their cues came from and address that problem.

If you want an adult that's trustworthy then you teach the child not to lie or shirk responsibility for the things they do and you teach them not to lie on others and be trouble makers.

Violence is a way of life. We are the only creatures on earth that have the ability to conjure up lies and use them to organize or destroy its own species. Nature is violent! Violence is the nature of being a predatory creature. It's how we get our food! We are about the only species on earth that abuses the privilege! Other creatures us it to establish who is going to be King of the Hill, (Peking Order), but we use it literally for entertainment and self-indulgence. We are the only creature on earth that takes it to such an extreme. We make movies about it, write books about it and engage in it as a means of settling disputes, (even if it's against the law). Hollywood gets a pass on this! Their products are in response to demand. They're not the cause! Instruction manual, maybe, but not the cause! Other species use violence to establish territory, (gangs do that), and engage in it as they train their offspring in survival tactics. Many predatory species will toy with other species, like wolves or coyotes chasing chickens, but rarely do you find any of these creatures attacking their own just for the heck of it! They are considered miscreants by the pack and are quickly ganged up on by the pack. (Street gangs do this too!) We have a natural penchant for violence because of our natural predatory nature. Fortunately, we have an IQ that allows us to control our violence and set standards of conduct as a society. We prefer to keep it within the realm of play acting on the screen instead of engaging in the real deal. We have chosen "Peace" over "War!" Our choice, unfortunately, is not necessarily the choice of the world and that makes us the prey to other predators and war becomes inevitable. The price of peace is measured in sacrifice and blood, not of our choosing, but at the choosing of others who would rob us of our peace and our place. Our choice is, do we wait for war to come to us or do we take it to them before they can harm us? In the past, we've allowed the evils imposed on other people to fester until their wars came to our soil and caused great harm. So far, we've been very lucky with our ability to defend ourselves. No nation conquered by us, in self defense, was kept as conquered territory for our personal gain. All lands were given back to their people and restored in better condition than it was when they attacked us. We left them with a better means of governance and they've lived in peace and prosperity ever since. We returned to them their own sovereignty and until we came along, that wasn't the practice.

The point to all of this is that this kind of thinking and compassion begins in the home with how we are raised as children and that responsibility falls on the shoulders of the parents, a fact that we have lost cognizance of! As a family, we are the shapers of our future, our destiny! As a family, we are responsible for instilling a loyalty towards our homeland and its roots in our children as the primary means of preserving our national heritage and our way of life. This too, has fallen to the wayside as we see more and more demonstrations of disloyalty towards this country as the product of these negligent parents hit the streets and do nothing but badmouth their own homeland and desecrate its image without any remorse or consideration at all, and nearly all of it is based on blatant lies perpetuated by nefarious individuals that have nothing but ill will towards this country; and worse of all, most are home grown, fully influenced by all the negative fanfare from home grown and foreign insurgents!

If we think of good and evil as a form of energy then we have positive energy vs negative energy, evil being the negative energy. Negativity is the absence of positive energy. Evil is the absence of good! "All evil needs to thrive is for good men to do nothing!" I've probably messed up the quote but you get my drift! The point I'm making is that good is something that has to be taught by good parenting. In the absence of good parenting, evil thrives! By nature, we are animals and therefore, without the influences of proper social upbringing, we act like animals, which is interpreted as evil since we are predatory by nature. There have been cases where children grew up in the jungles of India, and other places, where they were more or less adopted by simians or perhaps other compassionate creatures unknown and they all have one thing in common, they grew up without the influences of human social behavior and therefore acted like animals when encountered and all with the same fear of humans that wild animals demonstrate. I would conclude from that, that our ideology of what is right is something developed by human society and is taught by example, instruction and institutional educating. Our idea of what is right or wrong is not a natural born instinct. It is adopted behavior! As such, perpetuating those behaviors would rest first and foremost on the shoulders of the parents and, for the most part, parental responsibilities. Our Christian Bible encourages the assuming of those responsibilities and the church is the caretaker and perpetuator of society's accepted forms of conduct and character. That makes the church a very relevant player in the character of family and how it develops its offspring, as it bridges the gap of time and distance between families and other members of our society to create a unified standard that defines the character of our nation's future leaders. It is the only institution that shoulders that responsibility!

The bottom line is that family, its structure and its responsibilities to itself and the nation is the lifeblood of the nation without which we wither up and die away, as we are witnessing at this time and era. We have got to turn things around starting now because it is going to take several lifetimes before the turn around we start now, reaches Capitol Hill and saves the day and considering the state that we are currently in, in our decline, I'm not sure the turn-around is going to be timely enough.

CHAPTER IX

Sunday Sermon!

Science and the Bible agree that "in the beginning" there was nothing; just a great void! Science and the Bible both agree that man came from the mud of the earth, (Primordial Soup/"and God spit in the dirt and created man from the dust", or something to that effect). Science states that we are made up of the elements of the stars.

There are 118 natural elements in the Periodic Table and a few others that man has tinkered around and sort of created from a couple of the normal elements. I'm sure our concoctions probably exist somewhere in a natural state, perhaps even here but we just haven't found them yet.

Not a single one of these elements, by their self, or in combination, carry the characteristics of a life form or of having life; None of them! The earth, other planets, the stars, our oceans and our mountains are all made up of these 118+ elements and all are inanimate. All plants and animals are composed of these same "inanimate" elements! We are made up of these "inanimate" elements! Why then, are we animated and nothing else is?

It is because there is a third party involved that exists beyond the normal constraints of the laws of physics. In religion, we call it a soul! It is an energy life form that exists outside the realm of the physics that define our 118+ elements. This is what energizes our 118 elements into an animated state that we call life. When this energy leaves the body and relinquishes control of it, our body returns to its natural state of inanimate elements, if left to nature's design. "Dust thou art and unto dust thou shalt return!" Remember those words?

With all of this being the case, then it should also be obvious that the inanimate material that makes up our physical body is incapable of operating on its own. The soul, (living energy), has to push all the buttons necessary to animate our being and provide for its interaction with other beings and nature. Our brain and nervous system is the computer that it uses to do this. When our energy-being vacates the premises and quits punching the keys, we quit interacting and quit doing anything, except return to our natural state of raw, inanimate elements.

As Einstein said, energy cannot be destroyed. It can change forms and even then, remnants of it linger on! When we die, except for our inanimate state and the sudden beginning of decomp, there is no evidence of our energy life force having turned into something else like a flash of light or a new bit of matter. That means that our living energy has remained a living energy but it no longer inhabits the material body that we once recognized as our self in a mirror. The "we" that was once a material, animated creature that we looked at in the mirror is no longer that material, animated creature; we are now a form of energy with cognizance and abilities and conditions that are new to us as we take up a new life in another dimension not discernible by material life forms.

Life cannot be created in a chemistry lab or by rubbing two stones together. It can only be created by living life forms as it perpetuates the species. The soul creates more souls by using the material element we recognize as a life form, to procreate. Every time something procreates, it creates another soul as it imparts a part of its living energy into another material that contains living energy. Unless the two energies combine, life does not continue. We are energy beings and we use these bodies as incubators where we grow and learn and perpetuate the creation of other energy beings, to put it in non-religious, secular, scientific terms!

We, as spiritual beings, are fully dependent upon our bodies for the intellectual, interacting environment it provides for us to grow and develop. Eventually, either the body becomes no longer viable or we part company without reasons that are apparent to the living. It is the body that dies and which everybody mourns over, not us! We are continuing to live on but out of touch, for the most part. The point is that we are souls, (living energy), that occupy a body. The body isn't us, the soul is! The body is the soul's castle! The body dies and returns to the earth but we live on in a state that is a mystery to the living, even taboo! When God told Adam and Eve that they would die if they ate from that tree, He was talking about their soul, not their flesh and blood. The spirit of man has waned so much that we have begun to act more and more like animals and a lot less than like a saint. We are becoming more and more negative in our pursuits and attitudes every day. Remember, negative is the absence of positive, which is life, liberty and happiness! To me, this is a vetting of the soul's existence which then gives credence to the Christian's Bible which deals with the destiny of man's soul.

I have to disagree with many biblical scholars about the story of Adam and Eve. Just about everybody thinks of them as being the first and only humans to exist in his time because man was the last thing on God's list to be created. It says that He created Adam and Eve but what it doesn't say is that they were the only ones created or even if they were created first. The Bible contradicts the "lone creation" within the story itself! Other humans and other tribes were already in existence at the same time as Adam and Eve. The way I'm seeing it, is that Adam and Eve were probably the leaders of the many tribes that existed around that time and were looked up too as being connected. Adam and Eve were living metaphors for humanity. That's why all of humanity became condemned when they betrayed God's trust and sinned. It wasn't Adam and Eve that transgressed alone; it was all of humanity, just like we did to warrant Noah's flood! We all partook of some fruit, (behavior?), that we were told not too. Some scholars think that that fruit might have been an abundance of knowledge that we weren't prepared to handle and which would have done us more harm than good; that's why it was prohibited. When I hear that, I can't help but look at modern warfare and the repercussions from modern technology which we use without restraint. (Kids getting obese because of a lack of exercise caused by them having their nose in electronic games 24/7! Vehicle fatalities caused by people driving and texting instead of focusing on their driving, which they probably weren't too good at to begin with.)

If all of humanity transgressed and was therefore condemned, then all of those people's heirs have inherited that same damnation, "...for all have sinned and fallen short of the glory of God!" If that's all we have to look forward too then for what purpose do we live? If that's all there is too it then God should have totally destroyed us on that day and started over from scratch, but He didn't. He must surely have provided a way out for us; and He did! Throughout all of the prophesies, a deliverer is spoken of; a Messiah! Several other religions with similar tenets tell of the same possibility of redemption. Like with gangs, it's blood in, blood out! We, (Adam & Eve), severed our ties to God at the Garden of Eden and bonded with Satan in return for that "forbidden fruit". When God created man, He looked upon His creation as being perfected and called it good! Because a perfect being betrayed God, it would have to be a pure-blood, free of sin to break the curse that befell all of mankind. That's why the Immaculate Conception!

The Jewish faith calls the New Testament the Last Testament, as in Last Will and Testament. A will cannot be probated until the testator dies and then the will becomes executable. In this case, the will is open to whomever shows up and meets the specs for qualification. Christ died as the testator of the Last Will and Testament which willed to us forgiveness, redemption and a gift from that other tree, eternal life! This will is not forthright in this world but comes to us after this world has passed and a new world begins for us. Before the crucifixion and the affirmation of the will, the soul was awarded a place in paradise for being of righteous conduct as part of our commitment to our God. After the affirmation of the Last Will and Testament, our soul is awarded a place in God's Kingdom, whatever that might be, (and I'm not slighting it. It could be paradise times ten!) The main thing to me is that it will be a place of contentment, not discontent! It will be well worth any sacrifices we have to put up with in this lifetime to achieve a rightful place with God.

When we talk of redemption, we are not talking about flesh and blood; we are talking about the redemption of the soul, (living energy), whose existence is of the spiritual world. Our bodies, our flesh and blood is an outward appearance of the soul that occupies it. However the soul goes, so goes the body! Our communications with God is going to be on the soul's level of energy and energy exchanges for spiritual communications, not that of the body. The body is for the world's view, not God's. He sees the soul for what it is. The body is of little significance except for how the soul uses it to convey to others the story of God and redemption and sets the example for how to live like a family member of His Holiness, God! We are expected to bring honor to His House and give cause for others to want to enter in and become one with the Family. Membership is by invitation only! It's your decision!

Without "repentance" there can be no forgiveness and without forgiveness there is no inheritance from Christ's sacrifice. You remain condemned! Repentance is a renunciation of Satan's house and your heritage, which is everything that he has coming to him; from birth, we are his heirs. We recognize the fact that we are his heirs and heirs to his condemnations and will bear his burdens equally. The violations of the flesh are an outward expression of our attachment to his estate and his family. It is therefore crucial that we recognize and accept responsibility for this state of affairs and swear an oath to ourselves and to God that denounces that inheritance of Satan and swear to endeavor to serve God and abstain from future transgressions. This makes us eligible to be Christ's heirs. Our baptism is a declaration of the old self dying and a new self arising; we are born again – of the spirit! The old spirit, Satan's spirit as our navigator, is dead and gone and now we are born again with God's spirit as our navigator. We are on our way! I'm sounding like a preacher now but when you consider that we are living forms of energy then our salvation must come from a living form of energy.

This does not mean that we're instantly converted to sainthood! We still have a carnal body that is still prone to doing malicious things and if we get too arrogant, bad things will happen. Adam and Eve knew God personally to the same degree that we know other family members or a neighbor. They walked hand in hand through the Garden of Eden and discussed matters of the world and the universe. With all this kindred relationship, the Devil was still able to deceive them and bring down the fall of humanity. If he can do that to people who physically knew God, then don't think that he can't use you and your faith for foul purposes. Be on your toes because when you ditched him, you put a target on your back and sooner or later he's going to find you at your weakest moment and exploit it. Be strong in God!

Prayer and meditation is a spiritual thing. The thoughts run through our head but it is simply a readout of what our spirit/soul is contemplating and trying to communicate. I would refer you to the experiment spoken of on page 48 of this book which confirms the power of thought and prayer. If we can have an impact on the elements like that, and at that distance, then we should have no doubts about being able to reach the living energy that we call God.

Our New Testament faith insists that we treat others like we would want to be treated and love each other like family. It's amazing how many hypocrites we have here and around the world that shout "Peace, Peace" while engaging in nothing but violence and then have the audacity to attribute it to God. The Islamic Extremists/ISIS of today is one example but keep in mind that Christians and other, now peaceful, faiths also had their turn at evil. For me, a religion has to be able to stand on its own merits. If the proponents have to use force and/or intimidation to achieve a following then it isn't a religion, it's a cult and a dangerous one at that. There are two commandments that were given by Christ about how to do right by others and that is what sets us apart from most other faiths. There's no orders to run around torturing and killing people to perpetuate the faith. Instead, we are directed to live the faith and set such an example as so entice people to want to live and have a change of heart and become a part of the family. This assures that the people that come to the faith, and come to God, do it because of their love for God and their brethren and not because somebody's going to kill them if they don't. Persons taken by conquest can never be trusted to be loyal and if God wanted robots, he would have made robots! He wants "family!" He wants family with family ties and family loyalty. The universe serves at His command! He has no need for servants! He has angels, cherubs and seraphims to serve at His command! He wants family! He wants family members that think for themselves and don't have to be told what to do when something comes up! That's why He wants you to come to Him out of love for Him and His! If you love Him then you have no choice but to renounce any attachment to Satan and his family or his legacy, which is sin.

We couldn't do this while we were estranged from God! Christ built a bridge between us and God that the first of humanity burned. In your mind, have a conversation with Him and cross that bridge! We communicate with Him through thought and deed! Our deeds are our thoughts and intentions fully expressed. That's why He said, "Ye shall know them by their works!" He doesn't tell us that so that we sit in judgment of others and punish them through acts of coercion and intimidation but to be aware of them so that they cannot use them to deceive us or betray us with their follies! This allows us to act appropriately, set an example and thereby lead them to Christ and living right instead of staying the course that they have taken.

I will also say this, nobody has a right to sit in judgment of others, (beyond the requirements of man's laws), because we haven't a clue as to how God might be using them to work out the grand theme of things or impact somebody else's life in a positive manner. Judas was one of Christ's most beloved and Judas loved Christ but God had a need for him to do the unthinkable and so he was moved to fulfill the role that God needed him to fill. After he figured out what he had done, he committed suicide out of remorse. He thought he could force Christ's hand and show the world who Christ truly was and instead he fulfilled the scriptures that required Christ's sacrifice. Our only option in this life is to pray for others and fulfill our responsibilities of compassion and understanding, tempered by moderation and restraint.

Moderation and Restraint: When we spoil our kids rotten and save them from any responsibilities, they grow up expecting the world to kowtow to their every whim and need and to continue with the spoiling. Spoilage is spoilage and it destroys everything that it comes into contact with. Spoilage is taking the "compassion" to the extreme which is a violation of "in all things, do so in moderation". Part of being family is the expectation for each member of the family to carry their own weight and not be a burden to everybody else. Disabilities is the exception and it requires accommodation, not pampering, not spoiling! Having a disability means that we just have to blossom by some other means outside the norm and that is what makes us exceptional. If I can't hold a hammer to drive a nail then I'll get an air-gun to drive it for me! I was grounded from climbing steel for a living and so I learned to operate heavy equipment and drive truck. I no longer drive a truck or operate heavy equipment and so now I'm learning how to write this narrative! The way I look at it, if an obstacle gets in your way, you've got two ways of dealing with it, (well three if you count giving up as an option), you get some help to get rid of the obstacle or you go around it. I'm not one for asking for help with much of anything. If I can't tackle something head on then I'll tackle it from behind and if that doesn't work, I'll just keep nibbling around the edges until something breaks for me. Sometimes it just isn't your time to accomplish some things and you just have to move them to the back burner until God is ready for the issue to be resolved. Just don't quit and forget! Nobody in their right mind likes to punish their kids and we are restrained in the tasks that we give them to do, if any! These are things that have to be done and it is the parent's responsibility to do them in a timely fashion. If you don't do them, then you are acting counter to what most people want for their children, success and the ability to thrive! If you don't instill in them the virtues, values and abilities that they need to achieve those goals then you are damaging them and producing damaged goods, to their detriment. Work ethic is not inherited, it is a learned behavior! Honesty and compassion are not inherited traits, they are learned behavior! Parents are responsible for the transmittal of these characteristics into their children. We quit doing this in the late 50's, starting with just a few people but then like with all spoilage, it begins in one little spot and then spreads throughout the whole barrel if not put in check. The rotten apples need to be excised from society or their disease continues to spread until the whole barrel of apples, (our society), is destroyed. This is the role that the family unit plays in the good and welfare of our nation and its destiny and right now, that template has been compromised by a growing force of rotten apples! My father always said that when things go awry you quit what you're doing and go back to where you were getting things right and start all over again, and try not to repeat history.

CHAPTER X

Perspective on today's nation

The corruption that impregnates this nation's government from city hall to Capitol Hill is being exposed to the public light as one party attempts to drive the other party into obscurity through their defamation assaults on each other. Never before in our nation's history has there been such an abundance of corruption, legal and moral! All of it points to how much our nation has degenerated culturally, morally and ethically and it all points back to how the previous generations dropped the ball in how they raised their succeeding generations. We have become detached from our roots and moral social values which once made this a promised land. "We the People" have betrayed our own country by taking what our founders gave us for granted and didn't value it enough to protect it from the world or malevolent citizens that can't comprehend what constitutes a threat and what does not. There has been a deliberate severance of ties between the public and the church to the detriment of American society and the American culture of life, liberty and the pursuit of happiness. The abandonment of the church made headlines during the 60's as attendance took serious hits and as those conditions got worse, so did the social decline of this nation as its morals and ethics took a back seat to "if it feels good, do it" and where "make love, not war" became an excuse for loose and lascivious living and the abandonment of the traditional family template and its responsibilities to the destiny of this nation.

The American drug culture barely existed, if at all, prior to the mid 50's. The outbreak of our drug epidemic is fully owned by the 60's generation and their total rebellion against anything that represented our culture of the day. Totally disregarded was how they were going to impact the future of America and its destiny because none of them gave a crap! What set us apart from other countries was the freedom to act the fool without government charging us with treason for saying or doing what we want as criticism towards government or country. We had thousands that committed treason against this country when they fled to Canada and other countries to escape the draft or in protest against the Vietnam war; they got a pass where in other countries they would have been hunted down and shot or hanged. None of these miscreants have comprehended the significance of the slack that was cut them while others sacrificed their lives at the command of their government, dually elected by them and their parents. Some of you reading this are the "them" that I'm talking about and you know who you are. For the record, I'm not arguing that going to war in Vietnam was right. Our intent and objectives were honorable but I'm sure that if we had tried, we probably could have found a way, other than war, to bring about the changes their dissidents were seeking. Right now, it's hard too say what we could have done to improve their lives and their contentment with their form of governance.

You, (the American voter), had a bleeding heart for the fate of others and their persecution by a nefarious government or rebels that robbed them of any hope for survival and wanted us to do something and then when the government acted as necessary, because of the evil their adversaries presented, you sat in the grandstands and cast stones at the gladiators. There are caches of food in a number of countries that are rotting because the monsters that dominate those territories won't allow the distribution of that food except by force and you don't have the spine to commit to using force, let alone follow through. So your complaints about how the people are starving are muted by your lack of resolve to do what is necessary to achieve your original goal. We are a benevolent nation and are usually the first to step up and help people in need, (which is contrary to collegiate student assertions), but not everybody wants our help and others don't have a voice by which to say what they want or don't want and so we measure their conditions against our own standards representing what we think a quality way of life should be. Governments should represent the will of the people and so if a people has need of help, we should be able to offer our assistance, as a government, to their government and get a truthful representation of the people. We have offered our services to unfriendly nations that suffered from natural disasters only to be turned down. They might have needed the help but they didn't want our help, mostly because of indifference. They managed without us! We got involved in Vietnam because of the oppression of the people and the viciousness of their rulers and we bit off more than we could chew, in part because of indifference towards a commitment to win, (lack of resolve), because somebody else's problems were none of our concern. This is the attitude of an isolationist and the same attitude that precluded our involvement in World War II. All the vileness was somebody else's problem and we had no business getting involved, you the American voter said. It took it festering out of control until it nearly wiped us out before we decided enough is enough and even then we had fools demonstrating against getting involved in WWII while Japan was planning to finish us off. Fortunately, the majority of us were ticked off enough and determined enough to defend this country and the world from their aggression. After WWII came Korea where in we got involved in their civil war with the South fighting for freedom from oppression. Just like with Vietnam, the teardrops didn't have the backbone or resolve to follow through and so now we've got a divided Korea and the 49th parallel and a rogue regime that threatens world peace. Our politicians and diplomats figured they were smarter than the generals that knew the enemy and cut our intervention short. No belly for war! Our politicians and diplomats should have taken a hint from our populace behavior with Korea before committing us to Vietnam! One of the points I'm going to make here is that it isn't the soldiers that push the buttons and pull the strings; it's the politicians and diplomats and to whose tune do they try to dance to; the American voter! They're trolling for the votes that will keep them in office by attempting to placate the population's leanings. They stick their finger in the air and check which way the wind's blowing and that's the direction they're going to go. So, the buck stops with us, not the White House!

The political machine is an every day part of our lives. Party members and political aids silently join us or listen in on us at the barber shop, bar, beauty salon, ball game or wherever conversations freely take place and study the op/eds and the publishing of papers and magazines, watch the news and monitor social media to find out which way the winds are blowing and try to figure out where the majority of us stand on a variety of issues. You can then add to that the groups that write, petition or lobby our politicians to initiate a movement or a piece of legislation. Most politicians have files categorized by issue and so they can put their communications in the appropriate file according to pro or con to make it easy to keep a pulse on the issues. With every notable catastrophe or disaster the politicians and political hopefuls show up for photo-ops and declarations of concern, whether they're in a position to do anything or not. They do it to grab some limelight and center stage to stoke their image and garner political support at the polls, or perhaps among colleagues.

As one leading Democrat told me, when I questioned their ethics, it's all about winning. You can't do anything for your constituents if you can't get elected and so it's "no holds barred" when it comes to doing things to win and that includes slandering and maligning your opponent, making up lies and innuendos and doing whatever else is necessary to defeat your opponent. I fail to see how anybody adhering to this philosophy could look themselves in the mirror in the morning. As far as I'm concerned, the more a politician goes down this road the less trustworthy they are and the less trustworthy they'll be when it comes to serving you and telling you the truth about what is going on in their politics. The name of the game is going to be CYA, as far as they're concerned and they're going to tell you whatever they think you want to hear so long as they can stay in your good graces. Our safety is the ability to vet whatever we're being told, the sooner the better; and you don't vet by listening to somebody else's BS! You go to the source, or as close to the source as you can get and like a detective doing an investigation, you look for the evidence, not the gossip. Gossip is leads, not evidence! Most everything that goes on in the making of our history leaves a paper trail or money trail and that is what you look for. When you read an article on something, consider the source! All writers and all editors producing news reports, exposes, magazine articles, etc., are biased to one degree or another. We must take into consideration which way those authors and editors are biased, based on their products. We also have to take into consideration our own biases. Our source preferences are usually a good indicator of where our biases lay. I'm biased towards conservatism but that is tempered by humanitarian considerations. You can't be solely focused on only one aspect of life. You can't be a business machine that exploits humanity for personal gain at any expense and in total disregard for the destruction it does and you cannot be a benefactor at everybody else's expense! The ideology of socialism is to be everybody's benefactor at everybody else's expense, which forces humanity to the lowest common denominator. That's why in those countries that practice socialism you find a lower quality of life with less freedoms than what we take for granted. The only people that get to live a prosperous life under socialism are those of the higher echelon of the Peking Order of society as they glean for themselves what they want before anybody else is considered, (the cost of government)! On the surface, socialism sounds great but the reality is a depressed society that cannot thrive. These countries are the countries that jerk on your heart-strings over the plight of the people, as though their government had nothing to do with it. Like I've said before, it's the plight of the people that defines the integrity of their government. We thrive, for the most part, because we have, (or did have), a voice in our governance. If we're not done right then the opulence of office will be given to somebody else come election time! If you're addicted to one bias or another then you are bound to keep reelecting the same ideological pathology to office that you had before. If you watch history, you'll see that the pendulum of history keeps swinging from left to right and back to left as we go from one extreme to another. Infamous to these swings is the phrase, "It's time for change!" This idiot remark always shows its head before a swing in the status quo and it doesn't matter whether things are going right or wrong; there's always somebody that just cannot leave well enough alone and so they start the chant that we need change, whether it's needed or not!

Principles are the values that we apply to our lives and the decisions we make. Persons of few or low principles are the most likely to be dishonest and untrustworthy and refuse to let anything stand in the way of doing whatever it is that they want to do. "The End Justifies the Means" is a pretty good indicator of this kind of person, no matter how charismatic he or she might be. The trademark of a con artist is their ability to use their charisma to bait you into their con game. They don't let anything like principles get in their way! As voters, we, more often than not, neglect to watch for the principles that we embrace in the people we elect. If we are principless, then that's probably what we're going to elect into office and always to our detriment as such people are usually self-serving!

Political promises aren't worth the paper they're written on! It's not because the politician isn't sincere, (and he/she might not be), but it's because what they get done is contingent on the interactions of the other politicians that will have to be voting on whatever your politician is attempting. Those politicians, supposedly, are elected in accordance to the standards embraced by the people that elected them which are not necessarily going to be your standards, thereby creating a conflict of interest. This is where vote-trading comes into play. One politician promises to vote in favor of another politician's efforts if they will support theirs; a tit-for-tat obligation! That's why you see all kinds of obligations tacked onto pieces of legislation that have nothing to do with the original initiative. These extra curricular activities are often referred to as "Pork Barrel" legislation and "bringing home the pork!" This might be the norm for Capitol Hill but it tends to work very much to our detriment because the focus isn't on the good and welfare of the nation but rather on the solicitation of constituency votes; placating the voters of a particular leaning!

One of the things that we voters fail to acknowledge is that elected officials exist in a different world than the rest of us as they are privy to information and interactions with other governments and legal issues that we are not privy too. On a national level, we cannot be open in regard to a lot of issues because it tells the bad guys where our Achilles Heel is and how to exploit it and we don't want to tip our hand by letting them know what we know about them and whatever they might be up too. Contrary to what the media asserts, we do not have a right to know when that disclosure endangers our national security. The shortcomings and foibles of our politicians leave them open to blackmail and criminal prosecution if exposed and so withholding that information is a grey line between a need for prosecution and exposure versus secrecy for national security reasons. At this current time our nation has been caught with its pants down and totally exposed before the world; the mighty hero has fallen! This is what happens when you think you can thrive without the self-imposed restrictions of time proven principles and values that can sometimes be inconvenient! We've evolved from a restrictive society that observed certain minimal standards of conduct to a society that has little regard for such restrictions of personal and collective behavior. This has been the bane of our nation and its evolution ever since the 1920's. In the 60's, it went on steroids! Today we are seeing our degenerated values on full display before the world as the people we've elected display to the world who and what we are as individuals. The people we elect is our face and image before the world! Now I would implore you to look at the face your representative or senator is putting on display for all the world to judge, not just the nation. This is why "Character Matters"! We must have people of good principles and values to best represent our concerns in government.

Getting back to the world of the politician, we need to understand that conversations occur outside the public eye between allies and enemies alike. It is the confidence of these conversations that provide for the implementation of diplomacy in international relations. When leaders talk smack or lavish accolades, it's not just flippant diatribe, there's a reason behind their conversation and it usually is to placate their population and make themselves look good even if their intentions are malicious.

Kim Un is one of those that has painted himself into a corner. His population is completely isolated from all the rest of humanity and are forced to believe whatever he tells them and some of his stories are really off the wall. If you don't believe me, subscribe to his newsletter. It's like reading the Weekly Reader as written by a second grader! He brags to them about how he has gone to war against us and others and defeated them without getting a scratch. That's all they know and so they have no reason to not worship him as he demands. His father used to play this same game but he knew when to play us and call it quits as a way to get handouts for him and his country. Kim Un wasn't taught about how to play the game or when to call it quits and leverage benefits. He is pushing the envelope and he needs to figure a way to save face without looking like he's cowering before his enemies after making all his bold boastings. I don't think he accepts the idea that he would lose in an engagement with us and so he keeps escalating his threats in the hopes that we will back off in an effort to prevent a disaster. He also knows that when push comes to shove, China, Russia and Iran will have no problem siding against us if we execute a preemptive attack on him; "my enemy's enemy is my friend!"

Worse Case Scenario -

North Korea has had missile launch capabilities for a couple of decades now and the ability to put low altitude satellites into orbit. They have the technology, compliments of one of our past presidents and China! Kim Un has boasted about his ability to put a low altitude nuclear device into orbit over the United States with the intent of initiating a debilitating EMP over mid-America which would render all electronics useless. The EMP would fry everything electronic or electric related. Stop and consider that everything in today's world is dependent on electronics; transportation is dependent on computer electronics to function, all our communications is electronics dependent and the electric grid that we depend on for our survival, (A/C, refrigeration, lighting, traffic controls, grocery stores, drug stores and most home appliances and shop tools)! A properly placed EMP would literally put us back to the Stone Age in a matter of minutes. The casualty aftermath of such an occurrence would be in the millions and that, in and of itself, would produce a secondary aftermath as the inability to deal with the masses of bodies that would pile up, (because of no equipment by which to embalm or bury the bodies), we would be faced with massive epidemics caused by the diseases generated from the disaster.

Secondary to that would be the opportunity for two other enemies to take advantage of our disadvantage and commence an all out, boots on the ground assault upon mainland America. With no land communications, early warning and tracking information will be non-existent. This would allow an enemy to come ashore any place they wish and invade with little to no resistance. Even with an armed citizenry the resistance would be futile as there would be no way to coordinate a resistance.

During the second year of the Obama Administration and his budget cuts to the military, Russia intruded upon our airspace with nuclear bombers three times and territorial waters three times. These intrusions were a test of our national defense response times and capabilities! The planes were intercepted over the Rockies but the border intrusions by their Navy was another story. There were three Akita Class submarines involved. One set on the western boundary of our territorial waters of the mainland and another set on the eastern boundary of our territorial waters a little ways from Washington, DC. The third is of the greatest concern. It spent nearly a week inside our territorial waters within site of our Gulf Coast shores, cruising about without getting any response whatsoever. This is because the budget cuts implemented by the Democrats shut down a critical monitoring station on the west coast of Florida. The monitoring station is connected to a number of sensors placed throughout the Gulf of Mexico to track shipping, (including submarines), not only as a matter of national defense but for drug interdictions. It has a recording device that provides a printout of detected anomalies over a period of time. Normally, it would have been constantly checked on but because of budget cuts, it was left unattended for weeks at a time. Its records showed the presence of the sub but by the time word got out and got a response, the sub was well on its way home just east of the Caribbean area in International waters where we couldn't touch them.

If North Korea coordinated its efforts with Russia, its EMP would leave us fully vulnerable for a follow up by Russia and its allies. The Akita sub carried 32 nuclear missiles, (working from memory), capable of hitting anyplace in North America and each one of those missiles carried multiple warheads, I think it is something like 16 each. That is not something to be flippant about, especially when you consider Russia's propensity for taking advantage of other countries' weaknesses to attack and occupy. For the record, they've phased out the Akita and replaced it with the Akulu Class sub which, as I understand it, has stealth capabilities. If they took advantage of an orbital attack from North Korea and followed up with even more EMP explosions all over North America, we'd be beyond dead in the water. Putting boots on our soil would just be a matter of semantics! Our very structured infrastructure would provide them very convenient means of deployment all over the nation in a matter of hours or days and you can compound that problem with the fact that they have all the military capabilities that we have.

A lot of our critical ware is protected by Faraday Cage protection, such as military communications and commercial airlines but most civilian devices are not protected and there's no way to protect detection equipment because it has to be exposed in order to do its job of detecting, specifically radar, (like in weather radar, airport radar and marine radar).

This is a very real threat and we've demonstrated a propensity for negligence in protecting ourselves from this threat militarily, politically and diplomatically as we get involved in international affairs from an armchair viewpoint. I call it armchair viewpoint because we, as individuals, are not privy to all the conversations and understandings occurring behind closed doors with allies and enemies and we are not privy to what our cloak and dagger community is telling our leaders behind those closed doors, although that is changing because of technology like video chats, Skype, etc. Cellphones with cameras allow citizens on scene to broadcast live as events are going down from all over the world and when you start pasting the information together, they become like breadcrumbs leading you to the perpetrators of destiny. I call them perpetrators of destiny because they have the wealth to buy influence. George Soros is one of those people that has boasted about having the wealth to buy out little nations here and there and start wars to manipulate events to his advantage. He bragged about it! How much of it is true is up for grabs! Perhaps liberals are right about limiting the amount of wealth one individual should be allowed to retain as a matter of international security! But then, if we should do that to ourselves, who would limit other nation's from becoming the dominant factor and use us for a pawn? Everything has a flip side! Everything has karma and every action produces karma. Be careful about the karma you are creating!

The defense of our nation is what inspired the Declaration of Independence and our Constitution. That should tell you that our nation's defense should be our number one obligation when it comes to financing our government. I would put education a close second in our list of priorities because without knowledge we cannot protect ourselves from decay or conquest. To separate ourselves from our past is a sure way to commit suicide as a nation! That is why an education system is the first target for subversion by an enemy; be they domestic or foreign. You separate a people from lessons learned and they become putty in your hands; easily deceived and manipulated because they have nothing to measure the lies against! This is why you see a movement today to get rid of anything symbolic of the Confederacy and the Civil War. It is an attempt to erase the Democratic Party's role in championing slavery, secession from the union, segregation and Jim Crow Laws and breeding groups like the KKK, the Neo-Nazi movement and skinheads. They want you separated from that part of history so they can play the role of Knight in Shining Armor, coming to the rescue without their past catching up with them and causing questions to arise about their veracity. You erase the history and, with luck, you erase the bad karma you've sown. That is why Hitler got up to bat twice. He and his didn't succeed on the first try and so he engaged in acts of sedition against his own country to pave his way to the top for a second shot at the brass ring; and he succeeded! He led his people straight thru the gates of Hell! History is full of these incidents. We need to learn from our mistakes but if they are hidden from us for personal political or financial gain, then how can we learn from them? That's why the history of the Holocaust is deliberately kept alive and memorialized; so that we never forget. And yet, here we are today with people among us that proclaim to the world that it never happened and are hell-bent on burying their past so that they can repeat history! Stay vigilant!

Our nation is politically split between Democrats and Republicans with Democrats outnumbering the Republicans. None of the other parties have enough membership to warrant the use of our national election system for their primaries. That's why you don't see the same fanfare for them as you do the Democrats and Republicans. We Independents outnumber both parties and almost outnumber the two of them combined! Accept thru a letter writing initiative on our part as individuals, we don't have any influence over who either party chooses for their candidate/s of choice but we can most certainly make the difference when election time roles around. As an Independent, I figure, both parties have to take into consideration our leanings or risk the tide turning against them as we constitute the swing vote of the electoral process. Speaking for myself, I found the Democratic Party to be morally and ethically bankrupt where politics and leadership is concerned and, to me, it poses a clear and present danger to this nation's national security and the destiny that our founders had envisioned for us as a nation. The Republican Party comes in at a close second, not because it poses a danger to our national security but because it is a threat to the good and welfare of the nation because of its support of economic greed as though it is a good thing; it isn't! I'm neither a liberal or a conservative! I consider myself a pragmatic in that I look at issues as problems to be solved, not political tools to be used to manipulate people for personal gain in politics and wealth. I used to look to the Democratic Party as the problem solver for the Commoner but it has gone astray and forgotten the responsibilities that were endowed to them when their ancestors put their signatures on the Declaration of Independence with everybody else. They had an ideology that was indifferent to the one that went forward but they still committed to the same declarations and the Constitution and now they no longer want to be politically bound by that agreement because it keeps getting in the way of their salacious activities; the first conflict being the Civil War!

I used to do a little schmoozing and lobbying among our elected officials and as far as I'm concerned, none of them ran for office with ill intent on their minds. They were absolutely sincere in their intentions. It wasn't until they got caught up in the politics, (especially the water-cooler politics), of Capitol Hill that they hung up their halos and allowed their integrity to be compromised. Government and politics are creatures that have a life of their own, with a voracious appetite for the blood of anybody entering into its realm. This is why the intentions of candidates as expressed on their soap box carries very little weight with me. Once the doors close to their arena, these two monsters, (government and politics), take over and control everything and all voices become a cacophony of boastings and pleadings which disguise or even obliterate the intentions of the perpetrators. It's amazing that our nation gets anything done and a lot of the time, their actions are questionable. When one of our presidents was first elected to office, one of the first things he did as president was to sign an executive order, (out of spite), firing all cattle guards across the nation. Stupid is as stupid does! Cattle guards aren't people! They're a metal grate made from pieces of pipe that lay across the road to prevent cattle from wandering down the roadway and out of their pastures. Government doesn't make them! Government doesn't buy them! Government doesn't have anything to do with them! They are all privately owned, installed and maintained by the rancher! That's how stupid and irresponsible our leadership and Congress has become! This is an example of how our leaders use their offices for personal vendettas, not just in regard to politics but to attack individuals that they might have a grudge against. This is a violation of the people's trust! It is a betrayal of our trust in them to be trustworthy and my big problem with Main Street is that the Democrats generally give their own a pass on such misconduct because they don't want to spank their own cash cow! They can go about talking trash about their own country but God forbid somebody should talk smack about their cash cow, even if it's the truth! This is a problem for our country! We're not policing our own! There's an old cliché that says, clean up your own backyard before you go about trying to clean up somebody else's! With so much going on, its kind of hard to wrap our heads around this!

We hear a lot about tax reform and its impact on the "Middle Class". Please take note, they are not talking about the simple majority of the population that are "Commoners"! The opponents to the Trump reformations want to continue to butcher the wealthy and discourage their investing in America as though we are the only game in town. Again, stupidity reigns supreme! The economy and employment are both growing astronomically just with Trump's pursuit of the changes proposed. That should give everybody a hint that things are probably being done right! Apparently some of our leaders and "their" followers are stuck on stupid because their philosophies appear to be going to be proven wrong, and that takes from their credibility which, in turn, results in lost vote support! They don't want those reforms to so much as make it to first base, let alone pass, because it makes them look like fools and that will cost them votes. Protecting their image is more important to them than protecting this country! On the other hand, Republicans need to take note that Corporate America has never looked after the good and welfare of either the Middle Class or the Commoner. Its greed has obstructed the trickle down that they were expected to foment from the breaks they were cut and the handouts they got; didn't happen! The fat cats that caused the market crashes that caused the need for the bailouts got fatter as they pocketed the bailout money instead of improvising the "trickle down" intentions of DC, if there were any intentions at all! Talk's cheap! The good and welfare of the Middle Class and the Commoner are second fiddle to the greed of Corporate America, which includes Wall Street!

Here's another "stupid is as stupid does!" Wall Street, (which includes all other same style institutions), is little more than a print out of the financial transactions between lenders/investors and Corporate America. Much of the financing that banks engage in is underwritten by the insurance industry which uses your premiums for their investments. The interest earned is what is paying their costs when you file a claim. Banks and other lenders, invest the money entrusted to them by loaning it out or by buying up shares in various companies and becoming a silent partner in the business or industry. They either collect a share of the profits as a partner (dividends), or they collect loan payments (plus interest). This is what all those numbers are from the NASDAQ, Wall Street, Dow Jones, etc., etc! Everybody has a vested interest in what these numbers are doing because they are a reflection of how we are doing where business and industry is concerned. When those numbers tank, it is a reflection of product demand diminishing and that is caused by a loss of cash flow which is caused by wage losses. By the time our, (Commoners), situation hits Wall Street, we are already experiencing a recession as wages and jobs are cut so the fat cats can stay fat at our expense. When we can no longer keep the marketplace thriving then it gets reflected in the numbers on Wall Street and then that's when panic sets in; not when we started to go hungry! If Wall Street is a reflection of troubled times, then why are certain political leaders using it for a target and organizing hostile actions towards it? They are creating a band wagon for the irritated to hop on and vent their angers and thereby support that party's voting base and assure another successful election, even if that band wagon is based on a false narrative. The organizers of these charades know full well that Wall Street is not the culprit but it sure makes for an easy manipulation of the ignorant! Democrats are the people putting on this charade but it is Corporate America and its greed that is the culprit. Trump's problem is going to be getting Corporate America to share the wealth and not choke the life out of our economy by not supporting an appropriate influx of cash into the economy via the time clock on a per-capita basis. The cash flow of the economy is dependent upon how much the individual has to spend in the economy, not how big the payroll is! If, (for comparison's sake), a jug of milk costs $4.00 and the worker is only getting paid $1.00, then the economy is not going to work. The employer might be putting $4.00 into the economy because he has four workers but if none of those workers have $4.00 then how can they afford that jug of milk, alas, no cash flow is going to occur and the economy stays stagnant. This is what Trump has to fix. Tax reductions in and of themselves is not going to fix anything in the long run. It will be nice to have a near 100% employment rate but it will be totally meaningless if none of them can afford to meet the cost-of-living. The business could have a thousand employees but if all any of them have to their name is $1.00, there is still not going to be any cash flow to the economy by which to pay $4.00 for that jug of milk. We are still dead in the water! Minimum wage has good intentions but it is nothing more than a band aid, quick-fix for the larger problem of not sharing in the wealth. As stated before, wages are a commodity and as such, it becomes a part of the price of goods and services at the cash register; essentially reimbursing corporate from our pocket for what it pays us. Stupid is as stupid does! Under these conditions we cannot even hope to break even and that puts us in a pickle! How can we possibly get ahead or invest if we can't even break even?

Why do we have organizers telling us that we need to demand higher wages if we are not only going to be giving it all back at the cash register, we are going to be giving it back with interest? Technically, we are going more into the hole with every pay increase under the current income structure. For the Middle Class, this phenomena isn't that much of a problem because they are earning more than the cost-of-living as the Marketplace's cash registers are geared to their economic status, not ours (the Commoner's). We, (Commoners), are the lowest common denominator in our nation's socioeconomic structure in spite of being the most populous. This is not working! It is not working because the manipulators of our socioeconomic system robbed us of the ability to engage in secondary support venues which used to help us get ahead and make more purchases than we could with a single primary income source. Again, this was not and is not a problem for the Middle Class. It is solely owned by the Commoner who owns the majority impact on the market demand needed for the economy's survival! (We own the majority impact because we are the majority of the population, not because we are rich! We have more mouths to feed and therefore consume more consumables and white goods than the other two tiers of our socioeconomic structure and yet we have the least amount of money to do it with!) This is why the rebellion towards Corporate America and Trump! We Commoners don't see any addressing of our issues which goes way beyond just having a job or better pay; we need to see a closing of the wage gap that is killing America and "NO"; higher wages, as the labor union bandwagons keep shouting, is not the answer! Getting $4.00 is not going to buy you a $4.00 jug of milk because by the time you collect your $4.00 at the time clock the price of that jug of milk is going to be $5.00 and you're still going to be behind the eight ball; and the rest of the population is going to be pissed at you for jacking up the cost of living because they're all still getting the $1.00 and you've just made it five times harder to feed the kids for everybody else, and you've done it to no avail!

Corporate America artificially jacked the cost of living in order to profit off the labor transition that occurred during the 40's and 50's. It wasn't enough to exploit women as cheap labor, they wanted the money we made to get ahead by holding down a second job. That second income is what helped us to invest in America and create a booming economy but their greed didn't care. They elevated the cost-of-living until that second income became a necessity instead of an option and like bankers and used car salesmen, they came up with all kinds of creative excuses for doing it. Like with the politicians, morality and ethics fall to the wayside for the pursuit of riches at ours and the nation's expense! The expectation that Corporate America, (especially those companies moving back to America), will lower their profit margins by sharing more of the wealth, to me, is a pipe dream. I think that greed will continue to override common sense and the good and welfare of the nation; more specifically, the majority of the population, the Commoner!

Impoverishment is a great motivator for embracing evil as a means to an end! Remember: "The end justifies the means?" That's one of the politician's favorite go-to excuses for their sleazy form of politics. Wheeling and dealing in the drugs and prostitution and all the violence that comes with it is the lower income's alternative to crappy pay and price gouging. As long as those two incentives are functioning, we are going to have to deal with the cost of crime. Good guys are still in the majority but the gap is closing because nothing else is changing for the better. Substandard living conditions and lowered quality of life issues are going to continue to be fodder for the politicians and a byproduct of corporate greed heaped upon the backs of the American worker and the worst is yet to come. Manpower is quickly being replaced by robotics which can not only do more, more accurately than the common worker, but easily replaces hundreds of workers for little to nothing and zero labor costs. How is America going to deal with that hit to the economy?

    I don't care how robotic your factory or business is, somebody has to be able to buy your goods or services and that isn't going to happen if everybody is on the unemployment roles or worse! How do we get cash into the hands of the displaced in order to keep up the product demand that justifies a business's existence? Government issued base-pay, paychecks? In all probability, this is probably what we are going to be faced with and does that not make us some sort of socialistic state? Our own progress appears to be pushing us towards third world living conditions because the opportunity to expand our personal financial resources to get ahead is going to be stripped from us even more than it is now. Still want an open door policy on immigration? This transition is not fictional! It is already happening across America and around the world. Warehouses that used to be labor intensive are now becoming fully automated with only one or two people pushing the buttons to automatically sort, retrieve and load merchandise into the trucks and automated trucking is already being introduced to our transportation systems. We have robots acting as doctors as they hook up one doctor at one facility to another at another facility to provide improved diagnostics and procedures! We have drones now making deliveries and fighting wars! Drones take the personal connect from the act of combat which means that war is becoming impersonal and conducted without the feeling or regret that actual combatants feel. Will that cause future leaders from that type of environment to be insensitive about warfare? Will that incite careless behavior on our part? I'm 100% in favor of remote, unmanned warfare producing zero casualties on our side but I'm also concerned about how it is going to impact our mindsets about combat, combatants and willingness to go to war. I'm afraid we might be setting up a scenario where there is no incentive for observing restraint, morals or ethics two or three generations from now. We are already preparing the way by ditching the influence of church and religion in our society which is the perpetuator of long standing morals, principles and ethics at the community level.

There used to be a TV series in which the crew encountered a civilization that would exterminate specific numbers of their population as an appeasement to an enemy nation for appeasements they made in a tit-for-tat, impersonal game of warfare. Rather than face the horror of war, they would voluntarily execute projected casualties based on a war game tally. As we become more and more remotely associated with the horrors of war, will we too become insensitive to the horrors of war and become complacent about the loss of lives and property? We have video games that involve violent representations of warfare that are blamed for developing insensitivity towards killing other human beings; even to the extent that they are used for military training to desensitize combatants to killing so that they won't hesitate pulling the trigger and cause themselves to be killed first. I think that we should be wary of this desensitization process as being a possibility in future determinations about going to war and/or defending ourselves. The people we elect to office should have combat experience or at least some form of military experience so that they are sensitive about the stakes at risk and are not just armchair players. We have way too many Americans today that have never been in the arena and are perfectly satisfied with sitting in the peanut gallery throwing rocks at the gladiators and who, by the way, haven't even read the program, know who is playing on the field or what kind of game is being played. The worse of it is that I'm not especially targeting civilians with these comments, I'm targeting politicians who really don't care what the game is all about so long as they can get to throw some rocks at somebody. I would suggest to everybody that if you're going to jump on some bandwagon, be sure you know where it's taking you and be sure you can afford to pay for the ticket because sooner or later, somebody has got to pay the piper!

Government costs money! No big revelation there! Just consider the correlation between the loss of freedoms and responsibilities to government and the cost of government. The cost of government is representative of just how much of our personal lives and responsibilities we've handed over to government. Every time we give government an edict, it costs money and so how much of our lives has been abdicated to government is reflected in how much it has to tax us to pay for what we should be honorable enough to handle on our own. Not pointing any fingers but consider what party has the tax and spend reputation! The more they micromanage our personal lives and capitalistic participation, the more they are going to charge us for their services, wanted or not. Be careful what you wish for!

CHAPTER XI

Tying It All Together -

In case you didn't catch it, but I'm sure you did, throughout this little book everything carried common threads that each section merged back into the conversation. This is because nothing is isolated from anything else. Everything in the universe and our lives is tied together, sometimes up tight and sometimes so loose you don't notice it, but we are all tied together by this law of physics called "Cause and Effect!" Everything has an effect on something else and like ripples in a pond, that effect just keeps going on and on and after awhile it bounces off of something and starts tracing its steps right back to the source. Flippantly, we generally call this Karma! Karma is not relevant to time or distance and you cannot avoid it. Therefore we should be very careful about the seeds we sow in life because we're making the bed that we're going to have to lay in.

Aside from internal management, every piece of legislation is an abdication of responsibilities to the government and not especially to the people you voted for. As soon as a piece of legislation is passed, it becomes institutionalized by your government which takes away any personalization of its intent or deployment in the way of its administration. That means that it applies to everybody! Unfortunately, we've, or rather our previous generations, raised generations of adults who've taken their place in society who figure that their status exempts them from obedience to those laws, just like the common criminal. If you hand over the keys to the hen house to the fox, guess who is going to be having chicken three times a day! When one party dominates Capitol Hill, they're going to be eating "chicken" every day at our expense and when the fox is the only one you can complain too, guess where your complaint is going to go?

With the current Administration, (Trump and the GOP), the fox has exposed itself for what it is and to what extent it will go to protect its resources and fight to get the key back. It could care less about the farm or protecting the chickens. That's just a ruse to stay in power. Political rhetoric! The checkmate on their activity is, "are you better off now"? "Better off" doesn't mean the state is providing for you; it means you're capable of providing for yourself! State handouts always come with strings attached. We the voters, want accountability for every dime, nickel and penny we give the government and that means being able to itemize what those nickels and pennies went for. That accountability requires as close to full control over what you do with their handout as possible and so you have to give up the freedom of choice where it comes to spending its money. That's why you don't get to spend food stamps on just anything and why your medical care is minimal, nothing fancy or expensive. Beggars can't be choosers! Food stamps used to be tradeable merchandise among addicts trading stamps for cash so they could get their next fix. It still is! The government switched from stamps to an EBT card figuring that would stop the trading but it didn't. If anything, it made it more convenient as evidenced by the steadfast epidemic of drug addiction and addiction related hospitalizations. The problem with cracking down on how these expenditures are used is that its improved and enhanced restrictions usually tramples all over the lives of those who are innocent of wrong doing while the criminals/addicts continue to find new ways to exploit the system unscathed. Earning your own living gets rid of the inconveniences of government handouts. Those running the system are under pressure to get people back to work and instead of accomplishing that, the rolls have grown in spite of the restrictions and deterrents. In other words, economic growth failed because it didn't provide for the people and more and more people have had to go looking for help.

To reiterate previous statements, economic growth didn't occur because of both, a diminished growth in business and industry and business & industry's unreasonable exploitation of labor at the time clock which drove the economy down even more. Suffocating the economy creates unemployment and destroys the economic environment business and industry must have in order to survive.

As you can see, everybody's actions are tied together as they conform to the first law of physics, "Cause and Effect!"

If you are going to produce kids then you have an absolute responsibility as a parent to raise them up with values, principles and virtues that will shape their character and behavior for the rest of their lives and their influence on the world around them. That is a heavy responsibility that requires the complicity of two parents; one to earn a living and one to assure the development of the kids produced, which is a 24 hour a day job. There was a time where only one income was needed to meet minimal financial requirements for family survival and extra income resources were used to get ahead. Getting ahead was an option, not a necessity and so you didn't have to throw the kids under the bus to keep your heads above water. As we became less dependent on the land and more dependent on the time clock, options became necessity and so parental influence on child growth was compromised. We are seeing how that panned out with how our street cultures have gone down the toilet and have become bastions for crime and violence and the exploitation of others. This is evidence of a nation in decline! It also shows how we are all connected in such a way that the actions of one group can impact the outcome for another group. In this case, the demand of multiple income sources to make ends meet has impacted the parental influence over their kids to shape their character and behavior, casting that influence to the four winds. The street took the place of that parental influence and generation after generation, it has been allowed to fester and degrade the character of our communities and our government.

Our lives are all tied together with the same common thread of "cause and effect!" Everything we do has an impact on something else and to date, we've been rolling along doing our thing without giving it a thought. We've been "reactive" in our responsibilities instead of "proactive" and so instead of preventing forest fires we're spinning in circles trying to put out the fire we started with a bucket of water that's either empty or full of gasoline most of the time. We have got to stop being reactive to the bad things coming our way and start looking down the road and envisioning how what we do is going to impact things down the road. Cause and Effect! We need to be aware of what string we're jerking on before we jerk it.

We have an immigration problem! We're the source of that problem! We were negligent about enforcing the rules that were in place to prevent our situation from happening. We used to run back and forth across the southern border willie-nillie and share in experiences. Inland migration wasn't a big issue. Migratory farm workers would follow the harvest season and travel from state to state working the harvest and then go back to Mexico, where the cost-of-living was about $1/12^{th}$ what it is here, to live. Now we have a massive, illegal immigration into this country that is having an impact on every facet of American civilization. Is it because we're so great? Perhaps! But then maybe it's because things are that bad at where they are coming from. People prefer to cling to the things they have; "a bird in the hand is worth two in the bush!" They are accustomed to their homeland and customs and most would prefer to live their lives where they are if it wasn't for the corruption of government and criminals encroaching on their peace and tranquility. There's no way for the peasant to fix that problem and so circumstance push them into migration from family, friends and home and since we have open borders, why not here? We cannot take in the world and people that think that are flat out stupid and irresponsible towards themselves and their country. What needs fixed is the countries that they are running from and they can't do that alone.

Neither can we support the world any more than we can be the world's policeman and neither service is wanted by any of the world's nations as it is a smack against their sovereignty and their dignity. War is not a solution except in the matter of self defense. And with today's technologies in warfare, you better be proactive instead of cheap and lazy because it only takes seconds for things to go south in a really bad way. Teddy Roosevelt and Trump are both right in the assertion of "Peace through Strength!" You don't pick a fight with somebody that can whip your a**! Bad guys always pick fights that they think they can win, the weaker the better. That's why the image of strength is so important and that is the first edict of the forming of the union we call the United States. It was to combine our strengths as a matter of self defense against the tyranny and forces of others, especially Britain at the time. For some reason, certain among us think the bad guys have run away and we no longer need that image. They think that the bad guys think like we do and have the same honor and integrity that we do and are just "misunderstood!" There is no honor among thieves! To make the assumption that we are no better than the bad guys is a stupid, self-deprecating example of low self-esteem. It's a feeling that we have no business thinking that we are any better than anybody else which makes you just as despicable as the lowest of the lowlifes. We don't go around assaulting other countries willie-nillie and butchering the general population and we don't stuff Capitol Hill with the fine things of life while allowing 90% of the population to starve to death so that our leaders can take bubble baths, eat caviar and pick fights and blame it all on somebody else. My, how we've fallen!

We have lost our virtue! Virtue is honorable behavior. It's living a righteous lifestyle that others can look up to and want to emulate. The last Administration violated the trust of this nation, the world, our allies and of freedom itself as it betrayed all of the above in an attempt to buy off the world's enemy states to everybody's detriment. Bad guys can't be bought! They can't be bought because they have insatiable appetites for more, whether they need it or not. More power, more wealth, more recognition and it's for them, not their people. The people remain in bondage to malicious forces and threats of force as they go hungry and do without the conveniences that create a higher quality of life for the rest of the world. Because of the need to respect the sovereignty of other nations, we can't go in and fix the problem and the liberals that bellyache the most about it don't have the belly for what needs to be done; they figure if they give the bully our lunch money then he or she will go away and leave us and the others alone. Stupid notion! The bully is always present because he/she likes the dominance and easy pickings and if you're not going to put up a fight, why not pick you clean? I used to get bullied a lot when I was a kid and eventually my parents told me that I needed to stand up for myself and take on the bully or I was going to get my backside beat the next time I complained. The very next day, the same bully attempted to do his thing and I fought back, which surprised him since he was about four times bigger than me. He never bothered me or my brother and sister ever again. Dad explained to me that I might lose the fight but if I get a sandwich out his hide while he was pounding on me, he would remember that tangling with me would get him hurt as well and bullies don't like the pain and suffering any more than me.

Today's world -

The first year of the new Trump Administration has come to an end and he has brought about a great many changes from which our economy and culture has benefited but he is still a stranger to politics and naive about human nature.

For several decades, we the people, Democrat and Republican alike, have echoed that perhaps this country would be much better off if we had a businessman running this country like a business instead of the sewer of politicians that we had. Trump is that business person! Unfortunately for him, politics doesn't work like a business template, especially when it has a legacy of self-serving political corruption. We the people, have issues and problems that need to be solved but those issues and problems have become tools for the politicians to use to manipulate us and play politics with, for the purpose of running for office and staying in power, not for the good and welfare of the nation or anybody else.

I spoke of virtue and how our politicians and the political structure has become virtueless. What we are seeing playing out today on our political stage is a full blown exposure to just how virtueless our political society has become. "The end justifies the means" was a comment made by a Democrat, (while I was a Democrat). It is a self-justification for tossing one's virtues, honor, character and credibility in the garbage to achieve a political goal, usually that of getting elected or retaining office. It involves crawling in bed with all the wrong characters, contriving lies and innuendos to damage or destroy threats that may or may not exist, the perpetrators could care less. Just look at the garbage floating to the surface of the sewage in that septic tank we call Capitol Hill!

I will say this; I've never met a politician that did not have honorable intentions when they first ran for office. Like a new born Christian, they were ready to storm hell with a bucket of ice water!

Government, all governments, take on a life of their own once they are created and then it begins to consume anybody that dares to enter into its lair. You either play its game, its way or you die, (figuratively). Trump called this mess "the swamp!" I call it sewage! It is the place where evil conflicts with good and good intentions go to hell as the issues become lost in the chaos and buried by bad intentions.

We have a serious problem! We have two political parties that are literally at war with each other 24/7 and we don't have a way to reign them in, in regard to their malfeasances. If one party dominates Capitol Hill then we don't have a way to call the miscreants to task for their malfeasances because we have the fox guarding the chicken house.

In the definition of treason, it is the act of giving aid and comfort to an enemy or making war against the United States. That is the primary conditions looked at if somebody is going to charge somebody else with treason and you have to have three witnesses to the fact, an added insurance against the abuse of the act since it is a hanging offense. Not mentioned is the fact that sedition is also an act of treason but not with such serious a consequence.

During the fist two years of the Obama Administration, Capitol Hill was dominated by Democrats, not only in the White House and both Houses of Congress, but in subordinate governmental organizations.

We had two elected officials that committed felonies against the United States of America but because the Judicial branch was ideologically bought and paid for, they got a pass on their malfeasances. The Party protecting its own and betraying the country in behalf of the donkey! It seems nobody had a problem with it, not that it would have done any good anyway! You see, when an elected official commits an offense, they have to be impeached. Impeachment is about the same thing as a grand jury hearing except that it is the House of Representatives that serves as the Grand Jury instead of a body of twelve. If an indictment is found then it is handed over to the Senate for trial which decides guilt or innocence and the consequence, if not already spelled out in the law. I do believe that if one is found guilty of a felony and are relieved of their title then they also become subject to criminal prosecution by the Feds. If one Party holds the Senate or both houses then it fully controls the legal environment of Washington, DC. If there is a blatant criminal act that an elected official can be criminally charged and tried for then that is the aegis of the FBI. Once criminally charged, they are relieved of their title, (with pay, I presume), until the outcome is determined by trial. If found guilty of a felony, they can never hold a governmental position ever again, not even as a garbage collector! If the FBI is ideologically bought and paid for, then where is our protection from the nefarious acts of our elected politicians. It has become apparent that at least one of them has betrayed our trust in favor of the donkey, and overlooked the malfeasances of several elected officials while holding others of the opposition party accountable for theirs. That is obvious political bias, which is not supposed to happen within the ranks of the FBI, especially the upper echelons of the agency. Maybe the FBI should have politically oriented departments looking at the malfeasances of each other's parties and making prosecutorial determinations. At least then we wouldn't have malefactors being given a pass and their deeds swept under the rug in favor of one political party or the other.

    We need hard line enforcement against the misuse of power and authority for personal reasons, including the intent to use the office and position to deliberately do harm to targeted individuals or organizations. Politicians, especially Democrats, have a history of engaging in this kind of conduct. This should be a case of "one strike and your out!" A complaint, if verified, should call for an automatic impeachment proceeding to weigh whether the event did or did not occur and if it did, it should automatically go to trial before the Senate. But, here again, we've got a problem with political dominance over Capitol Hill and the disgrace of one Party favoring and protecting its own over the good and welfare of the people.

I'm beginning to think that the impeachment process should involve both Houses compiling a joint body of twelve, (evenly split), and if an impeachment complaint is found valid then it should go over to the Supreme Court for trial, instead of a biased Senate. In spite of liberalism and conservatism being sticking points for the Supreme Court, at least they are more intent on deciphering the letter of the law than kissing the backside of some party's derriere.

I would also like to see the Supreme Court nominees, appointed by the sitting president, have to go through a Constitutional vote of the people, like an Amendment to the Constitution, instead of a confirmation by the Senate, since the Senate cannot control its bias! A candidate's history should be open for public disclosure so that the public can decide whether a candidate is qualified to their standards or not. After all, we the people, are the ones that have to accept their decisions as our final fate.

The diatribes between politicians and candidates on the campaign trail and even on the House floors is out of control and unacceptable. Political behavior has become the epitome of lost virtues and lost honor. The lying, the slandering and contriving of false evidence to involve legal initiatives is unacceptable and those who engage in such behavior need to be banned from ever running for any government office ever again. It's one thing to pull an opponent's skeletons out of the closet for the world to see and quite another to promote allegations that are not based on truth or legitimate evidence. Persons that participate in such lies should be charged with perjury since they are making false government statements, (we the people being that government in this case), that involve criminal behavior, (prosecutable or not). Women coming out of the woodwork after thirty years and claiming to have been sexually assaulted in some way when it did not happen, should be prosecuted to the fullest extent of the law and the political figure that orchestrated the lie needs to prosecuted as a felon and never allowed to run for office ever again. Let's put a curb on the BS!

It should already be understood that government is not a business. Pay attention President Trump! It does not function like a business. You are limited in your powers; you are not a dictator like corporate heads are. That's why stumping candidates making all kinds of wild promises are lying through their teeth, especially those who've already held public office. You can promise your intentions and if you're a good leader, you might be able to convince the other politicians to follow your lead and see your intentions fulfilled. Beyond that, all the good intentions in the world are not going anywhere unless you can get everybody on board and you can bet your shirt that every single one of them are going to want to stick their finger in the pie and leave their mark on your initiative; which usually corrupts the crap out of the intent that the legislation began with.

Filibustering legislation by one party against another party has been the practice ever since day one but this needs changed as the practice is being abused by partisan politicians that put their politics ahead of the good and welfare of the country. The budgetary process needs to be filibuster proof! If we are going to be faced with a government shutdown then I propose that the first thing to go should be the politician's paychecks. If the government is shut down then obviously, nobody's working and if they are not going to work then we shouldn't have to pay them. At the very least, we should hold their checks in abeyance until the problems are resolved, the budget is passed and the government is up and running again.

Today's Democrats are betraying their country by giving preference to foreign nationals over the American People, "We the People!" That is a betrayal of America! Need it in writing? Take a look at one of the Democratic Representatives said on the House floor in early 2017, "To hell with America...!" That is a betrayal! That is disloyalty! That is not putting "America First", which, by the way, is a phrase that was coined by the Democrats and the Labor Unions back in the 80's, along with "buy American!" Strange how the politics change when the shoe is on the other foot!

Apparently the Dems want it so that all the Dems in New York, Chicago and LA get to run the Nation and everybody else gets to shut up! Isn't that interesting? The whole concept behind the Electoral College was to give everybody as equal a voice in our governance as possible, in other words, fly-over country gets to have a say too! We already have a problem with their, "it's my way or the highway" attitudes. That's why they're bucking up against Trump today. It's not about what's right or wrong, it's the "my way or the highway" attitude.

It's human nature to think that your thinking is right and you want to resist any contest to your way of thinking! I hate it when I discover I've been wrong about something but it's my own fault for not properly vetting the information that I based my opinion on. I get irked when some politician gets it wrong because he was lied to and his detractors accuse him of lying and then later on, we find out that it was his/her accusers that spoon fed him/her the lie through a third party or a weak link in his group. That's political corruption!

Commoners, politicians and the media all have one thing in common, emotionalism! We are generally on the receiving end of everything diabolical whether it's nature against us, government BS against us or our very selves shooting ourselves in the foot, which happens quite frequently. We easily empathize with those who are suffering other hardships and our emotions go into high gear. Emotionalism is what sells newspapers, not the stock exchange numbers, which most commoners can't make heads or tails of anyway. Look back on all the rhetoric that every politician has ever spewed forth and you'll find them playing on our emotions and our sympathies, not common sense! They use our issues and catastrophes to exploit our emotions to garner votes and electoral status. This makes the media and politicians bed partners! Whomever or whatever generates the biggest explosive story is what is going to be published by the media. That's why you see the media fanning the flames of dirty politics. It prolongs the drama and intensifies it and that sells more media time. The bigger the circulation, the more advertising you can get and the more you can charge for it.

It's a win/win for the media, printed or otherwise! So, the next time you start getting all emotional or hot-headed over something from the TV, radio or print, better check it out to see if you're being played and exploited before you jump on their bandwagon. The media has this addiction with taking liberties with their reporting and it isn't to get to the truth; if anything, it's to distort or hide the truth so as to promote an agenda and get everybody on board. It sells more papers and air time! If ever there was a cause for censorship, they are it! If you are going to publish lies then I think you should be held accountable. Repeating lies and promoting lies is just as bad but at least in those cases you can have reasonable deniability!

This is my emotion on DACA; illegal minors get to stay and their parents or guardians, not their entire clan dating all the way back to Noah. Adults that came here as children and have lived most of their lives here should get a free pass too! However, there's a caveat to those two categories; they all must apply for citizenship and jump through all the same hoops as any other foreigner to obtain citizenship.

Any foreigner, (after having passed a background check), that serves honorably in our armed forces should be fast tracked through to citizenship, especially if they went into combat and faced enemy fire in our behalf. Getting wounded by enemy fire, or friendly fire while in a fire-fight, should be an automatic qualifier for citizenship with all the benefits accorded any veteran and citizen.

All able-bodied Americans should have to serve at least two years of active duty in the armed forces. Nobody elected to national office should be allowed to hold office if they have no military experience under their belt. This does not mean that they have to go into combat but it does serve as a means to familiarize them with the military and how it functions and where its priorities lie, which is crucial to their elected office performance where military matters are concerned. Learning self-discipline and respect for our nation and its flag couldn't hurt either! It is preferred that they experience the cost of freedom for themselves and can relate to the sacrifices made for this country first hand, rather than relating to it as through some fairy tale or novel. I don't care if you see combat or not, if you've worn the uniform honorably and experienced the discipline of military life, even if it's from behind the desk, you will come away from the experience with a better understanding of yourself and your country and an improved self-discipline that will help you to achieve greater things in life because you'll now have the discipline necessary to go after them.

Today's generations have no loyalty to this country. That's why the gates are wide open to illegal immigration and why the Democrats are constantly engaging in a hard sell for wide open borders and all the evil that comes with it. Invite a bunch of them to dinner and put a glass of Kool-Aid in front of them and then inform them that one of the cocktails has been poisoned; let's see who goes ahead and drinks their Kool-Aid. Open borders are the same deal. The majority coming across might be OK but there's that one poisoned glass of Kool-Aid that's going to get somebody killed and the liberals want to roll the dice with your life at stake, not to mention all the other negatives coming along with the wide open borders ideology. The safety of this country and its resources must take precedence over foreign intrusions, legal or illegal. I guarantee you that if you sat all of them down to the dinner table and tell them that one of their plates is poisoned that nobody would be eating dinner. Ninety-nine plates are good but fear of the one would cause the rejection of all the rest. I concede the need to revamp our immigration process. I've believed that most of my life! I don't think that only the well heeled should be allowed into this country either. It's good for our country to have it that way but it's not fair to those who are left to deal with the conditions that the well off are fleeing from. Those deprived people, sooner or later, are going to rise up in rebellion against their oppressors and having an imbalance between the have's and the have-nots coming into this country agitates the problem that sooner or later will involve us.

I would propose that we work with those countries that we can count on as allies, to improve their way of life through education on politics and how to exploit resources for personal gain, (other than drugs), and how to engage in business operations like exporting/importing and employee management. Look at the countries that have learned how to exploit their resources for their own benefit and the benefit of their people and compare them to the countries that either refuse to to exploit their resources and/or interfere with the general population from exploiting their resources for personal gain. The only way to deal with them is to deprive their greed of gratification while the bounty of other countries improves their citizen's quality of life. I would include culture in that but our national culture has degraded in spite of having a higher quality of life than other countries!

On abortion, I'm against abortion! I have sympathy for the victims of sex crimes and can empathize with some of their desires for an abortion but I'm still against it. In the most basic of terms, you are murdering a human being explicitly for the convenience of a parent that doesn't want to be bothered by the pitter-patter of little feet in their life. In reference to the 118 element theology, life existed within the egg and the sperm before conception and became a new life form the second they merged. When they merged, a human being came into existence. With this in mind, I would be very careful about terminating a pregnancy unless the mother's life was at stake and then it becomes a matter of self-defense. As for partial-birth abortions, they are an absolute "NO!" They are an outright act of cold-blooded murder! In the old days when a woman carried a baby to full term, she was bluntly asked if she wanted to keep the baby or not. If she answered "NO", the physician would simply toss the infant in the waste can to die, or if he was merciful, would either suffocate it, break its neck or use some other method to kill it swiftly. When society came to realize the reality of this, the AG decided that he would start prosecuting doctors and the mothers for murder. When that happened, the medical community changed tactics. When the mother went into labor, they would reach in and kill the baby while it was still in the birthing canal. That way they could write down on their forms that the baby was still-born and not get charged with murder. I stand my ground and call this kind of abortion, cold-blooded murder. If there's going to be an abortion then, in my opinion, it needs to be done as soon after conception as possible, not a few weeks down the road at the convenience of its mother, (or father for that matter). That is the most humane way to go about it, but not the Christian way. Don't know about any of the other religions! Somebody's going to have to answer to God for their indiscretions, not man, and God isn't interested in opinions or excuses. That's my point of view on that end of the equation. Having a complete disregard for life and limb is why we now have a culture of drugs and a disregard for life and limb within the community that shows itself in the indiscriminate killings of innocent people as they go about their daily lives thinking they're safe where they are. It's a clear demonstration of a lack of conscience and that comes from how all too many of us are raising our kids. If you have no conscience then there's no way you can instill one in your offspring!

On street gangs; I think that street gangs, unless non-violent and benevolent, should be treated as home-grown terrorist organizations. Labor Union leaders are held responsible for any illegal activities taken by their members involving a labor dispute. I think gang leaders, should be held accountable for the activities of the gangs and that especially applies to the shot-callers. Any criminal facilitating criminal acts in or outside of a prison facility should be charged with a felony facilitation of the crimes traced back to him/her in addition to violations of interstate communications whether it be by phone or mail or computer. If they cannot refrain from outside activities then perhaps they should be placed in solitary confinement for the rest of their lives or until their sentence is completed. We keep hearing about how gang leaders continue to operate from behind bars, even call the shots on people they want to get rid of. That BS needs the screeching brakes applied to it!

Our jails and prisons come under the heading "Department of Corrections!" With an 80% to 87% recidivism rate, I don't think the "correcting" part of the program is working! When you watch the exposes of what goes on inside the prisons, there's little room for doubt about the poor performance of our prison system where correcting behavior is concerned. You hear very little about some of the prisons that actually are engaging in corrective programs that are meeting with some success but the results are still pretty pitiful and the public is the one being put in harm's way when there is little to no effort to change the behavior, character and mind set of released prisoners. Even boot-camp programs have a difficult road to hoe with results that are not that much better. Complicating the process is society's refusal to give the convict a second chance. I can't blame society for the hesitancy but unless we come up with some way of facilitating reintegration into society and the encouragement of changed behavior and values, we are not ever going to have anything turn around. Even if somebody is fully rehabbed the stigma attached to them and their history is going to constantly haunt them and cause them to be self conscious about their status and behavior. That might be what it takes for them to stay on the straight and narrow or it could be a causative factor for returning to their past way of doing things. Those people that have been institutionalized for most of their lives usually have great difficulty in adjusting to community life outside the prison with some deliberately committing crimes to get re-incarcerated because they just can no longer function on their own without somebody telling them what to do and when to do it. Pavlovian lifestyles! Fixing all these problems is going to take intense studying, sorting out and revamping of our correctional institutions. It will save us thousands of lives and billions of dollars to take the time to get things right. With all this being said, there's no arguing about the fact that some people need caged forever. They are literally clinical sociopaths that will never conform to society's rules of law and order and pose a threat to everybody's life and limb.

Do I favor executions? Yes, but with reservations. I think that murderers that exhibit no conscience whatsoever about what they've done need to be put down as a matter of self-defense for the public. This would include guns for hire, serial-killers and sociopathic killers. None of these people have any regard for the value of anybody else's life. The heinousness of the crime should probably be a consideration to determine whether a person is sociopathic in their disregard for another's life. I just watched a documentary where a young mother was murdered. She was taken to a remote field with her baby in her arms and murdered. She fell to her back still clutching the baby which died from the elements while lying on its dead mothers breast. The murderer showed no remorse at all, not in his act nor in his trial. He deserved the needle! He is an unrepentant sociopath. In cases where there is mutual violence, like a bar-room brawl or heated argument where emotions get out of control, I'm good with prison time and depending on the case, any release should be conditional upon an evaluation of whether the community's temperament has cooled down enough to prevent any further altercations. Hostilities should warrant relocation to another area of the country where the perpetrator is an unknown, but at the same time, this person should be monitored to see how he or she is coping, (are they returning to the old behavior? Do they need technical assistance like in education or community services?) Once you've been labeled a criminal the stigma sticks. You're first on the list for anything going wrong and based on statistics, justifiably so! It's up to the individual to climb their own mountain and repatriate themselves to society and prove themselves and its going to be an uphill battle because of the distrust they've sown.

======000000======

The Character of Politics, USA -

Liberals vs Conservatives! Ever wonder what their motivational forces are?

I don't think I've ever met a politician that had ill intent when they first ran for office but some most definitely had dysfunctional ideologies within their id. Democrats have repeatedly mouthed their ideology of being smarter than everybody else, especially over the Republicans, and therefore it should be their way or the highway. This was underscored during the Obama Administration when Party Leaders called the voters "ignorant" and "stupid". ("Low information voters!:) They then bucked up against anything the Republican Party wanted to accomplish, (Republicans do this too), for America because it didn't fit their defective ideology, further underscoring their assessment of themselves as being the absolute in politics and intellect. (Neither Party is doing us any favors by engaging in this behavior which intensifies partisan politics over the good and welfare of the nation.) They could care less about how much their agendas cost and so spend like our pockets are an endless supply of cash for anything they want to do. This is the Party that contains elements within it that advocate doing away with the affirmed and old aged for financial reasons. They support euthanasia, (remember Dr. Kevorkian and how members of the Party supported his efforts), which adds to my observation about their posture on the affirmed and the aged. (They chide the Republicans for calling them death squads!) The Democratic Party is socially driven and gets the majority of its support from the working class/Commoners. The working class/Commoner is generally overcome from trying to survive and tends to take things at face value because they don't have the time to bury their heads in politics and be chasing down leads to get to the facts. They put all their eggs in the leadership's basket and trust them to be honest with them. Bad idea!

Conservatives are at the other end of the spectrum and focus on the finances instead of the social needs of the population. They tell you to teach a man how to fish instead of feeding him. They then set up shop and sell the lessons and the fishing gear without thinking about the fact that the person doesn't have the money to buy their goods and services because they can't fish! Amazing! This is why you see the pendulum of time swing back and forth from one extreme to another. The American voter is fickle as hell; loyalty is not one of his/her virtues as is demonstrated by their attacks on the American flag and partiality towards violence and other criminal activities as they fall prey to their emotionalism and political propaganda. The waters are so muddied that you have to be a magician to get to the truth, the whole truth and nothing but the truth!

As pointed out before, the primary reason our states came together as a nation was for mutual self-defense. No one state had the power to defend itself against any onslaught from an enemy nation, most specifically the armies and navies of Great Britain which were oppressing us. That must be the dominant budgetary item on our list of priorities. I would say that paying Congress would be second on our list of priorities but our first Congress was compiled of volunteers that devoted their time and wealth to building a Nation capable of self-sustenance. The cost of taking care of governmental responsibilities was the driving force for allocating incomes to elected officials. Once again, we've allowed the fox to guard the chicken house. They have full authority to allocate better pay for themselves as they wish without any meaningful push back by any other authority. Everything else on the agenda comes after those two items. The Executives of the world allot for themselves lucrative pay scales, (to the detriment of the working class), and so our politicians are put out by the fact that they earn much less than their counter parts in private industry. I would remind you politicians that your position was to be a voluntary position which meant you survived on your own finances with only a token amount from your employer, "We the People!" I realize that times have changed and your positions have become full time jobs but you err when you put your paychecks ahead of what your focus should be on, the good and welfare of the nation; not the donkey, not the pachyderm, not relatives, friends or supporters. The majority picked you because your theme fit theirs but that does not exonerate you from serving one and all. That's where life gets unbalanced and things go to hell in a hand basket!

We are not the world's honey pot! Our resources are not infinite! We cannot afford to play wet-nurse to the world as evidenced by our own inability to make the payments on our own debts! The lands of this nation belonged to the American Indian and all others are here by reason of conquest and immigration. To the detriment of the Native American, we took his lands by force and made this country our own new Promised Land but it soon became apparent to our early immigrants, (which took over this country), that we had to control the immigration coming into this country because of finite resources. It was from their wisdom that our immigration policies were orchestrated. Now we hear the narrative that we can afford to accept the influx of illegal immigrants. Spoiler Alert: We can't even make the payments on our National Dept, which is in the trillions of dollars. The deficit is what we "LACK" in being able to make the minimal payment on our debt to our nation's creditors. It is not the debt and it is not the payment! It is how much our budget is falling short of keeping our financial promises! We are not paying down our debt because of this and our tax system ties us all in physically in being responsible for paying this debt if it is called in. We have fiat currency which is nothing more than a promissory note that promises that we can produce whatever we need to produce to make good on our IOU's. We are the Producers, not business and industry. "We the People" are the ones responsible for turning the wrench that produces the product that is needed to fulfill the IOU contract. Sounds like an abdication to slavery to me!

There's two ways to make good on currency; by the fulfillment of the Promissory Note or with actual commodities/collateral, like gold, that already exists and is backing up the dollar. There needs to be some disclosure here. We had stockpiles of gold, silver and other valuable metals and gems to back up our currency until Nixon, a Republican, took us off of "representative" currency and put us on "fiat" currency. What has happened to that gold and valuables since we've been on "fiat" currency, that is based on productivity instead of raw collateral? If we went back to collateralized currency, would it be there to guarantee our currency or has it been pilfered? Something to ponder about!!

Most disgusting is how political interests have turned from addressing the good and welfare of the nation and its people to focusing on partisan politics and slandering and maligning opposition politicians and their parties, (with made up BS too), to do nothing but muddy the waters and divide the nation. "A house divided against itself cannot stand!" This is happening because we are not holding the people we elect to office accountable for their conduct. If you participated in electing this misconduct then you are responsible for controlling their misconduct, not the opposition! We cannot be controlled by conservatives alone any more than we can be controlled by liberals alone. They have to balance out against each other but with one common goal, the good and welfare (a Constitutional mandate), of the Nation and its People. What we, as voters, have to watch is being influenced by all the propaganda muddying the waters as the politicians and lobbyists vie for power, wealth and permanency and play us to accomplish that end.

To wit: The Republicans latched on to Bill Clinton's improprieties and pushed the impeachment. As far as I'm concerned it wasn't worth all the hoopla because it distracted us from what they should have been focused on which was his declassification of our missile guidance system technology and facilitating its sale to the Chinese to help their space program. I don't think North Korea's advancements in their ballistic missile program was accidentally coincidental to the sale of the guidance system technology to the Chinese. They are allies!

To wit: The Steele dossier, allegedly bought and paid for by the Clintons and the Democratic Party and now we have found out that it was completely orchestrated by the Clintons and the Democratic Party feeding bogus information to the British spy, Mr. Steele. That is political corruption and totally designed to compromise the presidency and this nation. As far as I'm concerned, that's treason, chargeable or not! Hillary utilized private servers for personal and governmental communications which conveniently provided access to classified governmental information, (put there by Hillary), which compromised the integrity of the election and National Security, which the Russians were quick to exploit in their effort to upset our apple cart and turn our election into a sham and make us the laughing stock of the world. Our gullibility and eagerness to trash each other's political party and the candidates, fed right into Russia's efforts to destabilize and discredit our electoral process and compromise its credibility before the world and our voters. We put getting dirt on each other ahead of our integrity so that we could trash each other's candidate enough so that nobody would vote for him/her. That is not how we are supposed to select a leader. We were creating false character impressions and labeling each other with them and that leads to electing failed leaders. It seems that it has become next to impossible to find a candidate that is of moral character and behavior and that is what we should be screening our candidates for before they ever file to run.

I was a Trump supporter for a reason. For decades we've been talking about having a business person run this country like a business instead of sticking with career politicians that worship their Party's mascot and its political platform over being loyal to America.

We haven't been able to get a clean bill through Congress for generations because of everybody using the back door to get dispensations or regulations that they can't get any other way. They make amendments contrived to appear like they're interlinked so that they can piggyback into law on a piece of legitimate legislation.

One of their more popular ways of shooting down a piece of legislation is to introduce the poison pill. That is an amendment or proposal that the opposition knows the proponents do not want and will cause them to vote against their own bill. This is what the Democrats are using DACA for currently. They proposed to apply it to only a few hundred thousand. Trump proposed to apply it to about one and half million. They weren't expecting that and so they bucked that to slide in some other junk proposals that they knew he would not approve. Of course, they then chase that with a bunch of propaganda making him look like the bad dog! That's how today's politics are played! Why? Because we have instant communications today! It's like we're right there participating in the action when in reality, we've all but lost our voice in the management of our country.

We are a sympathetic people and the plight of others tugs heavily on our heart-strings but at some point you've got to draw a line or you're going to be completely overwhelmed by the plights of other nations that fall short of doing their people right. Democratic Party leaders know that we have trouble saying "NO" because most of us Commoners know what it's like to have to live in poverty and have to struggle for survival with no hope in sight. They know that playing on that sympathy will garner support and votes and guarantee them time in the spotlight and in power and position, which makes them money.

We have another passion; we like money! Nature used to be our means of survival and we didn't need money. Commodities was our money; commodities that we produced with our own hands from whatever we got from nature. We transitioned during the 20th Century from surviving off of nature to having to survive off of money which we get from the time clock which is controlled by business and industry. When Republicans hit the campaign trail, their focus is on economics and balancing the books and building up business and industry as the ends all resolution. To do that we need to generate money and focus on where it goes so that we have somebody to tax and that is what creates a tax base. Since the Commoner has little to nothing, we have to look for the deep pockets to minimize the impact on the "little people", to quote a certain Democrat.

Have no doubts, business and industry is in business to make money for themselves, not everybody else. Remove the incentive to be in business and there's no reason to be in business any more and so the doors close, the tax base dries up, people become unemployed and that results in a deficit in the the nation's economic cash flow which inspires more closures and more depression. For some reason, this is a concept that Democrats cannot grasp at any level, either that or they just choose to ignore it! Because the economy runs on cash flow, Corporate America seems to be under the impression that our world rotates around business and industry and their prosperity. News flash, it doesn't! You are in a symbiotic relationship with labor whether you like it or not and that puts us all in the same boat! The Commoner makes up the majority of the population and therefore makes up the majority of the kind of product demand that is needed to keep the exchange of goods and services for cash alive and thriving. Corporate America cannot exist without our spending our paychecks . Two things can suppress market demand; not getting paid enough to meet the cost of living and being priced out of the market at the cash register. High wages is not the answer. As pointed out before, the cost of labor is paid for at the cash register. Let that soak in! You cannot get ahead of the eight ball based on wages alone. What we lack in meeting the cost of living is called the wage gap. It is the difference between what we have to pay out at the cash register for our survival needs and what those same entities pay us at the time clock. Merged into the price we pay at the cash register is Corporate America's profit margin. Lowering prices comes out of that profit margin and Corporate America's board of directors and investors, (which is us either directly or indirectly), isn't going to stand for that. When we put money into a savings account, an insurance plan or some retirement product, we look for the maximum interest payable to get the most bang for our buck. We're paying for that "bang for the buck" in the price of goods and services which might be pricing us out of the marketplace and that, of course, suppresses the economy and the commodity market which feeds us. We're between a rock and a hard place.

The Republican Party pushes business and industry because that provides us with more people getting paychecks and that feeds the economy between the time clock and the cash register which feeds the economy of Wall Street! What Corporate America and the Republicans seem to forget is that the cash flow that makes for a vibrant economy and a thriving marketplace is contingent upon how much the individual worker takes home and that without that outflow of wages, their income and prosperity dies. The only fix for this is minimizing the profit margins to cause the worker's paycheck to better meet the cost-of-living.

We had a boon time during the 50's as we rebounded from the Great Depression and World War II. Up through that time most of us thrived off of one income source per household; in the sense that we were able to pay the bills with some ice cream money left over. To get ahead and get into the position of buying homes, cars and other high ticket items, we would take on secondary employment which gave us money to put into savings and investments which nourished business and industry growth. Our country began to prosper dramatically but business and industry couldn't leave well enough alone. They began to jack the prices at the cash register until those second jobs became a necessity for breaking even, not getting ahead. We're in the 21st century now and its hallmark is that we need more than two or three jobs just to break even and that's disastrous for the single parent household and most families. Our commodity marketplace is compliant with the Middle Class's income-related cash flow and that crucifies the survivability of the Commoner which, in turn, suppresses the economy's cash flow and market demand.

We cannot survive without the cooperation of business and industry and business and industry cannot survive without ours. That's just the way it is! Government, on the other hand, is a parasite! It takes and takes without giving much of anything in return. Business and Industry is government's dinner plate. It sucks its money from all of us, especially we Commoners. Business and industry isn't going to take the hit. They pay their taxes but those taxes are calculated into the cost of their goods and services and that's what we pay at the cash register, which is further taxed. In other words, we are paying their taxes at the cash register. Democrat's theme song is "tax the crap out of them!"

They keep selling you on the idea that business and industry is paying the taxes and we shouldn't have to pay anything because we just don't make that kind of money. Wake up! Everything they get duped out of, you pay for at the cash register, and/or reduced wages, or lost jobs due to automation, as they maximize their profit margins at your expense. I think the biggest sucker punch is how time after time, the Democratic Party dupes people into believing that their raising the income taxes for business and industry is really something! Business and Industry and most of the rich, do not pay income taxes so tax away. Look at your tax form and find out what constitutes "income". It's what is paid out in hourly wages or salaries. I haven't seen a store or factory walking up to the entrance and punching the time clock. They don't pay an income tax. You've been duped! They survive off of "Capital Gaines". That is their source of income, not the time clock. So the next time you hear your favorite politician chanting "jack their income taxes", know you're being played.

As for business and industry, the world does not orbit around you. You are dependent on the consumer and the Commoner is the chief consumer. There are two different marketplaces. The consumer's marketplace, (my terminology), is where commodities are sold to be consumed. (There's also a commodity market for Wall Street which bids on projected crop and livestock estimates.) The other marketplace is where business and industry is financed on a public level. We recognize that market every day in the news as Wall Street, the Dow Jones, etc. Business and industry pawn or sell shares in their business to obtain the finances needed to expand or meet costs on a special project. All those numbers are a reflection of those stock values, how much trading is going on and how well the business and industry is doing. It has nothing to do with the economy that the rest of us live in, other than reflect how much business we're doing with whom. When they talk about how the economy is doing, they're talking about how well THEIR economy is doing, not ours. They all figure that if they're prospering then all's well at the bottom of the food chain! All them green arrows pointing up is their uptick in business and credit value (rating). The bigger the numbers the more valuable their portfolio is and the easier it is for them to borrow money at lower rates. Those dollar signs are what lenders and buyers are laying out cash for in regard to the respective business or industry. Some of that money comes from our personal pockets in the way of insurance premiums, retirement plans and savings accounts. What we pay into them is invested in those numbers you see coming from Wall Street. It is the interest from those investments that the insurance industry and banks use as income. (It's called Capital Gains!) They lose money – our rates go up! This is a rather loose overview of what is going on with your money when it's out of your sight.

America borrows money too! In 2011, our credit rating took a dump and was downgraded. Guess which Party was managing our financial affairs when that happened! That meant that our payments on our debt went up and so did the penalties on our deficit. (Deficit is how much we are falling short on making the minimum payment on our nation's credit card!) Just think about what would happen if you did that with your credit card! How much business would you do with somebody that can't pay their bills? Even drug dealers don't tolerate that kind of behavior! That's the position we've been put in by not paying attention to our financial affairs and constantly catering to the wants and needs of other countries and their people, including illegal immigrants. This is why so many of us wanted a business person to take over the leadership of this nation instead of another politician. Grant you, this is a scary proposition because we are all used to the same old same old and are used to seeing things dickered over for years before anything gets done and even then what gets done is screwed up because we have too many cooks in the kitchen.

Business and industry apparently cannot be allowed to run free reign because their profit margins supersede the good and welfare of the nation as evidenced by their abandonment of this country to pursue better profit margins on foreign soil. Business and labor are no longer two separate entities and the two of them need to accept this. We cannot exist without business and industry and business and industry cannot exist without us as consumers and producers. We are a part of the balance sheet and if we come up short so does business and industry, which, by the way, has the ultimate control over the health of the economy. Republicans and Democrats need to come to the realization that the world doesn't just rotate around one or the other. Business and industry, represented by Republicans, with their focus on finances, must balance against the humanitarianism of American society as represented by the Democratic Party. Neither has a blank check to do whatever it wants to do and "We the People" need to enforce that! When we elect somebody to office we are hiring them to work for us in the managing of our nation's affairs. We need to treat them as employees, (with respect due their office and status, of course)! We do not hire them to lie, cheat, steal or murder in our name and we do not hire them to misrepresent our character and beliefs before the world and embarrass us abroad.

I would suggest that first of all, shed the bias and just look at the image that our nation is projecting to the world and consider what you would be looking at if you were an outsider listening in. Today is the day of the Internet; get on your computer and start surfing the internet of other nations and get the opinions straight from the horse's mouth. All nations and cities abroad have media outlets and most produce email type newsletters to their people and the world and even have online publications that can be accessed. That's where you're going to find what other people really think, not the propaganda that the Party bosses and their compliant media sources are spewing forth!

The media isn't what it used to be. Nearly all editors are Democrats. That's a conflict of interest right there! Nearly all reporters are Democrats and that compounds the bias. If the driver and his/her cheerleaders are all in on the same bandwagon and don't care where it's headed and you're jumping on board, you deserve what you get! Over the years, I've found that one Party running the White House and the other Party narrowly controlling Congress, seems to get us the best performance from both. That's not going to happen this time because there's way too much animosity between the two camps.

Trump took the electoral college vote and that gave him the election. The response by Democrats was absolutely pathetic and unacceptable, even for kindergartners. Their antics were an absolute embarrassment to this country! The first thing out of their mouths was "lets get rid of the electoral college!" This is what happens when you put ignorant people into leadership positions. Their justification was the few thousand votes that gave them the majority. What they don't tell anybody is that those few extra thousands of votes came from concentrated populations of Democrats in Democratic districts, totally disproportional to the rest of the population of the United States. Contrary to what Trump and his supporters would like you to believe, he carried nearly every county in the country but it was by the hair of his chinny chin chin! Most of the counties carried him by a little over 50% of the popular vote. He, by no means, received a mandate. This debate over the validity of the electoral college comes from ignorance. Without it, the only people that would have a voice in the affairs of our government would be those living in the high population areas of the country which are mostly Democratic. That's why they were bouncing off the wall. All those extra votes came from LA, and the New York/Massachusetts area and even then it was only from about three different counties. I guess the Democratic Party thinks that all presidents should be elected by those few counties and nobody else gets to have a say! They spewed out their propaganda and an ignorant population went for it hook, line and sinker! They were quick to jump on the bandwagon even if it meant that their voices would be silenced forever. This is what happens when you sleep through government, civics and history class. The Electoral College is the only thing that gives voters living in fly-over country equal representation in our electoral process. As demonstrated this last election, apparently Democrats don't give a crap whether fly over country gets representation or not, if it costs them an election.

I, for one, am sick and tired of the sore losers and deliberate obstruction of government by the losers instead of knuckling down and making sure we all have a voice in our government's business. This business of "It's My Way or the Highway" has to stop. I've been around a long time and I've yet to see any of them walk on water yet or part the Red Sea so as to justify an "It's My Way or the Highway" attitude!

One of the tricks Democratic "Get out the Vote" operations utilize is volunteering as a non-partisan operation to provide rides to the polling places and then they only show up for Democrats to give them rides to the poles. They disenfranchise all the Republicans by leaving them sit until the polls close. This is just another form of voter fraud and Party workers take pride in their acts of corruption. You'll never see a single Democratic voter call them on this! Apparently honesty isn't one of their member's virtues! If you are a liberal reading this, do you see how your official's behavior reflects on you and your character on a personal level?

Headlines playing politics:

Headline by "Business Insider": "Your retirement plan probably funds nuclear weapons" as posted on the Internet. Political intent: Trying to alarm the anti-nuke crowd and stir the pot to generate more readership which sells ad space! 3/6/2018

Point: There isn't a single dollar bill in this country that hasn't passed through the hands of one of the drug cartels and most will test positive for contact with cocaine; should we accuse those spending those dollar bills of being complicit in the nation's drug trafficking? What they're referring to is where the investors are investing the premiums you pay, like with Lockheed Martin or Boeing, etc. These same people trying to raise your ire seem to have no problem with places like North Korea or Iran developing nuclear weapons but God forbid we should take care of our own.

New York Times: "Trump Hates the Trade Deficit. Most Economists Don't. 3/6/2018

Political suggestion: Economists like the deficit and therefore Trump, a Republican, is wrong about attacking the deficit; ie: Republicans are wrong and the implication is to vote Democrat. Trade Deficit isn't the same as our Debt. In order for our "Fiat" currency to remain stable, we have to be able to trade tit-for-tat with other countries. The more we fall short of doing that, the less valuable our "Fiat" currency becomes on the world market and the more we have to pay for goods and services and in interest. It means that we are spending more money than we are bringing in, in our business dealings with the rest of the world and that does add to our national debt which we already can't pay down! Just for the record, the "New York Times" is considered a "liberal" rag and a staunch supporter of the Democratic Party agendas. There used to be a joke that went around, "I must have good credit, I owe everybody!" Apparently the Time's economists have this point of view too!

Market Watch- "Dow futures over 100 points higher, lifted by Korea talks. 3/6/2018; Headline tends to support Trump efforts to get NK to the bargaining table. A bump for Republicans. I know what Trump is attempting to do but what I am unsure of is how well he knows Kim Un. Kim Un's father used to play this game to get concessions from us and other players but he knew where to stop. I'm not that sure about Kim Un's savvy. He wants to fill his father's shoes and prove himself better than his father but he also has to be careful to not paint himself into a corner where he can't save face before his people who are completely devoid of any knowledge of the rest of the world, (except for some of the elites of their society), and think that their way of life is superior to that of the rest of the world because of what Kim Un keeps telling them. He is their only source of information. In one of his newsletters to his people, he bragged about how he went to war against us and prevailed. We all know that this is BS but this is the only information that country's commoners are exposed to. He's been putting on a show for his people and attempting to stare us down in front of his people to build their respect for him and animosity and fear towards us. I'm worried that at some point he'll have painted himself into a corner with his braggadocio and will have to put up or shut up and his lack of experience and abundance of ego could go very bad for him, his people and the world. Hints that Kim Un might be willing to come to the bargaining table is a very good sign that things could be turning around. I'm expecting Trump will attempt to provide Un with some means of saving face while still achieving denuclearization. That would be a win/win!

Television bulletin:

EU raises stakes for Trump with tariffs targeting GOP heartland

The European Union is preparing punitive tariffs on iconic U.S. brands produced in key Republican constituencies, raising political pressure on President Donald Trump to ditch his plans for taxing steel and aluminum imports while attacking the Republican constituency.

Bloomberg 3/6/2018

President's Response: (Paraphrased) "If you want to play that game then let's see what you think about a prohibition against Mercedes,

BMW and other European products being sold in the US!" Point being that they already do discriminate against American products such as food and appliances and flat out prohibit their sales in their countries, not just tax them. This is the behavior Trump is targeting and we hear the cacophony of moans and groans coming from both sides of the isle from people that want to play it safe and keep taking the shafting we've been getting!

The Hollywood Reporter -

"Conservative Media Attacks 'Phony,' 'Divisive' Oscar Broadcast."
Media is accused of being liberally biased. This is that media's response! It can't prove that it isn't and so it attempts to shift the focus.

If you don't think the politicians aren't playing you, consider this; In the early 80's the Labor Unions were trying to organize the illegal immigrants that were working the vineyards and orchards of California and couldn't get any of them to sign up. They threatened to blow the whistle on them and have them deported if they didn't sign up and the organizers were told where they could stuff it. When they couldn't get the signatures the unions initiated the Allard Pesticide scare figuring there'd be a panic that would shut down the California grape and fruit industry and get all the illegals laid off as business took a dump. The FDA was quick to rebuff the claims and scare tactics.

The Labor Unions and the Democratic Party are in bed together. The Unions needed the political support of the Party in order to counter the malicious behavior and political power of Corporate America and the Democratic Party needed the voting bloc that organized labor represented and so it was a good marriage of assets. When the Allard scare backfired, the Democratic Party took up the chant that the illegals were sucking up American jobs and driving down wages as alleged by the labor unions. The Labor Unions and the Democratic Party took up the chant, "Buy American" and make America prosperous again". Imagine that!

Today, those very same people are chanting the exact opposite. What happened to all that damage they were alleging that the illegals were doing to our nation? Looks to me like it was a posture of convenience to rally votes around, not that they really believed that there was a problem. After all, aren't these same people singing just the opposite today? What changed? What changed is that the Republicans have taken up the banner for controlling immigration and so the Democrats are deliberately bucking the movement because they know they can play on your sympathies and play you like a fiddle and get you to forget what they were chanting in the 80's. These are the same people that spat on our returning troops from Vietnam and called them "Baby Killers" and abused the crap out of them when they came home. Now, all of a sudden, they pretend to hail all soldiers while they stab them in the back at the budget table thinking that nobody will notice. They've stuck their fingers in the air to see which way the wind is blowing and the winds of time now favor the veteran; so now they pretend to be on the veteran's band wagon so they can play innocent and pull in the votes. Fair weather simpaticos! I don't know about you but I'd rather go face to face with an opponent with full knowledge of what to expect than have somebody pretend to have my back and stab me in it and violate my trust!

The Democratic Party has been losing support and so over the past couple of decades or so, has been courting the votes of convicted criminals by championing their reinstatement of rights, (deserved or not), and acting like they don't have that pathway available to them through appropriate legal procedures. They have been championing voting rights for non-citizens (illegal aliens), which is in violation of national security. Illegals are not allowed to vote to prevent foreign agents and governments from influencing our elections. Once again, Democrats ragging on foreign influences on our elections out of one corner of their mouth and championing it out of the other corner of their mouth!". They have chosen to gleefully harbor fugitives and offer safe sanctuary to them and have openly, on the floor of the House proclaimed "to hell with America!" We had a president whose church of choice openly derided America and proclaimed from the pulpit, "God

Damn America". He supported that behavior and then claimed to be a patriot. Patriotism is loyalty to your country and the leadership of the Democratic Party has done nothing but do its best to put this country on the back burner and allow this country to be overridden by foreign insurgents, their cultures and beliefs and their ideologies and that is mostly because most of them are Anti-Christ and Anti-Christianity; thus the penchant for the infusion of Sharia Law over our own. They want us to feed the world and invite the world in when we can't even feed or house, our own! They tell their constituents that we can afford to do these things when we can't even make the payments on our national debt, let alone pay down the national debt and people bite on it. They use our sympathies to play us. They know that a lot of us have had to survive on little or nothing and therefore know what it's like and so we have sympathy for anybody else down and out like we've been. They stuff the world into that little box and play on our passions, not because it's the right thing to do but because they use that to con us into voting for them. They use our passions to herd us to the voting booth in support of their false outcries. This is why, generation after generation, their promises do not bring forth fruit! Instead of doing away with poverty, it increases as demonstrated by the increases in the numbers of people that have to fall back on food stamps and other forms of public assistance or go to private non-profits for assistance. If things were getting better under their watch then the poverty numbers wouldn't be growing. Conservatives are right in that observation! I'm going to point out something else though, if the conservative ideology was doing so great then we wouldn't have had a need for government intervention in the first place. There's a constant battle between the "haves" and the "have-nots" which defines humanity's "Pecking Order!" It is the wealthy that are able to buy power and influence.

In ancient times, it wasn't uncommon for a miscreant to rob others like a common thief until he had enough wealth to pay others to do it for him and that allowed him to grow into power and influence. We do the same thing today except that we are a little more sophisticated about it. It's when somebody drops their veil of sophistication and their misdeeds come to light that they get called on their behavior. Alas, that is what politics has become all about, not the good and welfare of the nation, a nation that was supposed to be set apart from all other nations in how our hierarchy was to be achieved and maintained. I've found that those who squawk the loudest are usually the guilty culprits; they think they know what is going on because they've already been there, done that and they think that everybody else thinks just like them. Where does that leave us? We're supposed to be the followers and our leaders are supposed to be setting the examples and I don't see anything that I would care to brag on, let alone follow.

Trump has a history of bankruptcies but he managed to get his act together and put himself in the black. He also had a history of one tryst after another which resulted in a couple of divorces with the last tryst occurring during his candidacy and after being married for a third time, at least that's what the Democrats want us to believe. She's still with him so I guess they've figured things out. Take note on how the liberals want to make a big thing of this while giving their god and goddess, Bill and Hillary Clinton, a pass on their trysts and malfeasances. Why do they do this? Because they know that the Commoner will rally around the whipping post and that turns into votes and political support! You can see what happens when the shoe is on somebody else's foot, alas Trump! Dishonest perspectives, no core values! The Kennedy's had their trysts and from what I've been able to glean from history, nearly every president we've had, had something going on in the background. Fortunately for us, they were dignified enough to keep theirs low profile and mostly off the radar. Their image was important to them, in part because such behavior was frowned upon and they realized that their image was also the image of this country and represented the world's perception of who and what we are as a people. Notice that today's politicians could give a flip about what they present to the world! That is a symptom of a nation in decline and it seems we're all on board with it.

Everything that is wrong with the world and this nation began in the home and with how somebody's parents raised them, generation after generation. Evil is a do-nothing disease! Do nothing and it will fester and flourish and prevail towards everybody's detriment. It doesn't need encouragement or fertilizer to flourish and take over the Garden of Life! It comes naturally! Righteousness, (good character and proper behavior), requires nurturing, training and constant care or it will be destroyed by the weeds. That is what parenting is all about; taking care of their seed and seeing to it that they are properly nurtured and cared for so that something comes forth that you can be proud of and expect only the best.

The media reflects to us, and the world, a picture of our garden and what has become of it and today's picture is nothing to be proud of. There is a total lack of honest introspect as individuals, in our political beliefs and the affairs of our society. We yell and scream about the violence in our streets and schools and totally ignore the fact that these miscreants are a product of our values and examples as set forth by the way we've lived our lives before others, especially our own kids. They are an expression of the values that we set forth. If our lives was fraught with ungodly lifestyles, (disharmony, lying, cheating, stealing, hotheadedness, violence and other irrational behaviors), then that is what the next generation has to learn from. This is not the responsibility of a school or government. It is the parent's responsibility. The bad things in life already exist all around us in abundance. The good things in life are sitting on the shelf and have to be chosen for the taking. Being good, with very, very few exceptions, does not come naturally and I cannot stress that enough. It is taught behavior! That is what sets civilized society apart from a barbaric society; it is how the rules of civilized behavior are embraced and passed down through informal teachings and leading by example. Evil is when we act like animals, (even worse than animals), instead of creatures of a higher order that can distinguish between what is evil and what is right. (Post Script: Even the truth can be used to do evil! Sometimes we'd do well too keep our mouth shut and let things work themselves out!) Righteousness does not ever seek to cloak itself with the mantle of evil but evil works very hard to always cloak itself with the mantle of righteousness. That's why thieves and murderers try to convince themselves that what they do is justified. Righteous behavior exonerates and they want to be exonerated and allowed to do whatever they want. They want to be righteous but they don't want to quit what they are doing!

The rules we live by as a society defines our perspective of what righteousness is. Looking at our society today, it looks like all the rules have been thrown out the window! There is an all out assault on Christians and Christianity by leaders in government and by one commoner against another. We had a Supreme Court decision many years ago that came to the conclusion that "Freedom of Religion" also meant "Freedom FROM Religion" in total disregard for the second line in that Amendment which says, "nor prohibit the free practice thereof"! We have lost all loyalties to our own country as demonstrated by the allowing of the desecration of the American flag as a matter of "Free Speech" instead of being an act of "Sedition" that is often times associated with acts of insurrection, both of which are acts of treason. When a sitting House member, of her own volition, can go and lie to an enemy state to subvert the activities of a presidential administration and the Congress with impunity, that is a loss of loyalty! That is a betrayal of our country! No matter what the excuse, it is an act of treason as far as I'm concerned! That is not patriotism! When a seated member of Congress can facilitate the "harboring of a fugitive" and collude with an enemy state to do it, that is a betrayal of our country and an act of disloyalty. That is not patriotism! Those are examples of rebellion against our country from within the highest positions of leadership which has inspired similar behavior among impressionable youth who now engage in acts of violence against our country, our government and society itself. And they do so with the protection of the courts who can no longer distinguish between right or wrong; they just go with the flow! Because this behavior is different from the behavior of the past, this type of behavior is accepted as being "progressive" behavior and perfectly legitimate. Once again, we have "evil" wanting to don the cloak of "righteousness" so that it can justify itself in its own mind and feel righteous. You can dress yourself up to look like a sheep all you want but in the end, you're just a wolf in sheep's clothing! We have reached a stage in our society where people vote for or against a politician because of Party affiliation instead of what they stand for as demonstrated by their behavior; or as the Bible says: "Ye shall know them by their works!"

The whole theme of the Democratic Party, as far as I'm concerned, was to look after the little guy, ie: the Commoner, and protect him/her from the big, bad ogre: business and industry, and their Republican Party and their malfeasances against the people! Somehow, somewhere down the line, things have morphed into an unimaginable mess with the Donkey heading up a charity ball, instead of managing the legal relations between labor and industry/business. Again, and this is a personal opinion, the Party needs fixed and its leadership needs replaced. We need leaders that are focused on fixing problems instead of putting on a show of total opposition to other leaders simply because they are of an opposition party representing the other half of the equation. Charity comes with a price tag. If I can't feed my family then I for darn sure cannot afford to be feeding outsiders, especially when doing so would put me in the same boat with them so that we can all go down together. Nothing is solved and matters are only made worse. Most of the deprivation we suffer from is, in a way, caused by the malfeasances of business and industry, not because they broke the law but because of their disregard for how they interact with and impact the economy that the rest of us are relegated to living in. The nature of this nation's economics has changed from being dependent on nature to being dependent on their time clock and cash register and their refusal to recognize this and accept responsibility for this relationship has done us great harm and the facilitation of this situation rests with both sides of the isle. The one wants to keep facilitating hand outs and the other wants to focus on fatter profit margins to the detriment of the economy. It is not higher wages or lower prices that facilitates a healthier economy, (which facilitates a higher standard of living), it is the shrinking of the wage gap that facilitates a healthy economy.

Getting back to the point, raising a family, in spite of what "progressives" proclaim and assert, takes two parents; and, as Hillary pointed out, it also "takes a village". Two parents cannot be effectively involved in raising their family if the home is void of the parents as the result of everybody having to work to break even within the cost-of-living created by business and industry. I'm not saying that a single parent cannot effectively raise the kids but it most certainly stacks the odds against that happening and if you have parents that are of questionable character then the odds get ten-fold worse.

As for, "it takes a village", it does! Kids/young people, interact with the community as they become more mobile and more mature and their reaction to the actions of other citizens/businesses, provides lessons in behavior and social conduct. I don't know of many kids, if any, that haven't engaged in some degree of shop lifting. If you're attentive, you can see it happen during the course of the day as you walk around shopping and you can see little toddlers and grade-schoolers as they are allowed to run amok in the store. Eventually, one of them is going to slip something in the pocket or eat it in the isle. In the old days, (my generation), if you were caught, you were publicly embarrassed by being taken to the side and have the pockets emptied of the store's goods and then your parents were called over or notified at home where you got crucified! It generally only took one incident to change that developing character trait. How a business conducts its business tells the consumer how to do business with that business, if any at all. When you, as a young person with a head full of mush, engage with shady business characters, it's not hard to get the impression that that is how you do business. It's not "barter", it's thievery! They learn! When scandalous politicians get caught and put on display, what does that tell our young people about the character of those who serve in government? Image is very important! It sets the standards! Remember the "Ponzi Scheme?" Charles Ponzi, for whom it is named after, was raised by somebody and that somebody, (which includes the community), was responsible for developing his character with its values, ethics and virtues from which his behavior evolved. His scheme wasn't something new. The practice was written about during the 1700's and 1800's as well. My question is, how was he raised? What was his rearing environment like? What were the values, morals and ethics of his parents and the community within which he was raised? Who did he "hang out" with as he was growing up and learning about the value of his labors and currency? This would be an interesting study? He grew up in poverty and hung out with unseemly characters according to some of the history facts. He was always working some kind of quick buck scheme to escape the kind of life that he was brought up in. Pretty much the same kind of incentives that inspire today's drug dealers, quick and easy money!

This is where democracy and freedom begins; it begins with the family and the passing down of family values and traditions. It begins with parents teaching their offspring to take responsibility for what needs to be done without having to be told. It begins with parents teaching their offspring to take responsibility for the things they do, "own it!" It begins with parents teaching kids the need for honesty, honor, loyalty and earned respect; not forced respect. It begins with parents taking an interest in their kids lives enough to know whether they are straying from the family creed or not.

One of the values that has been lost is the value of the Christian religion and its Bible in stabilizing and strengthening the family and the community whether you're a regular church goer or not. The Bible and its guidance is unwavering and unchanging and that acts like a set of railroad tracks for civilization to travel along on without much of a conflict. Who can argue with commandments like, "love thy neighbor as thyself?" It means treat each other like family. (But then, on the other hand, I've known some families that I wouldn't want to be any where near!) It commands us to "Do unto others as you would have them do unto you!" If those two commandments alone were followed by everybody, just imagine what the world would be like. Sharing and helping would happen without question. It advocates doing right by each other and with that not only as a goal of the family, and being taught by the family to their kids, where can you possibly go wrong? As much as the atheists hate the very concept of there being a God and chalk it off to superstition, it's pretty hard to deny the impact that emphasis on following the guidelines of modern biblical teachings can have on those who embrace them and reflect them to others. The hold-back is that there are a lot of people who want to wear the halo but have no intention of embracing the concept of brotherly love. The church also has a heavy burden to bear because of its sordid past and failure to follow the teachings of Christ which has blackened the name and image of the church. You cannot un-write history! (At least honest people can't!) All you can do is take the now and start over, doing it right! Love for the Christian way of life is the only requirement and incentive for joining the church and practicing the faith. It fails me to understand why this would scare the crap out of non-believers/atheists so much that they would foster terrorist acts against a church and look for ways to twist government and the courts to attack and prevent the free practice of such a faith! Even if it is all superstition, it has a righteous impact on our communities.

I think the hardest part about parenting is that nobody wants to be the bad guy. We all want to be the loving, passionate, never-gets-mad parent and leave the enforcer role up to the other one. The roles have to be balanced. The hardest part of this is taking on a leadership role which also transposes to the kids as they watch and learn, in turn, how to be leaders. If kids aren't learning how to take care of the home by doing chores, etc., then how are they going to figure out how to take care of themselves when they get out on their own? If they don't learn that things in life have to be earned then how are they going to grow up not expecting everything to be handed to them?

My father always told me that when things get screwed up, you stop what you're doing and you go back to where things weren't screwed up and start over and make sure you don't repeat history. Use the knowledge you now have to fix the error of your ways.

We've changed how we treat women and view their roles in society. That's a good thing! The Bible says she was created to be "an help-mate". That's not a slave or somebody's possession or a pet to be treated like a dog. She's your right arm. The Bible established the man as the leader/head of household to reflect God's role with creation and His family. Being designated a leader doesn't make you a dictator. You are supposed to reflect God's image and God's role in the universe but within the family and the community. That means you treat everybody with love and respect and that is especially true for wife and kids. Even if we embrace this standard we still have to clean up our social mess which means continuing to crack down on spouse abuse, (which women have joined the ranks as well), and child abuse/neglect.

Divorces can be reduced by following some old fashioned rules that helped to prevent people from getting together for all the wrong reasons. They kept their pants zipped and legs crossed and, under the parents tutelage and chaperoning, hung out together and got to know each other first. Dating was for figuring out where each other's interests laid and if they had a chemistry together. After that, things got serious. I can't say for sure if this behavior was the exception or the practice but it does warrant taking note of because today's generations have no problem eating desert first and giving way to infatuation, thinking it's love. They hook up and then a year or two later, after they've got some dependents, they can't stand the sight of each other and they start acting out and eventually get a divorce, nasty more often than not, and the kids get caught in the crossfire because everybody is wrapped up in themselves. Mom and Dad is going to be their mom and dad forever and it's not by their choice and then they get emotionally ripped apart as they're forced to choose between parents or feel dissed by one or the other that takes off on a lam.

What has changed since the early 20th Century was an overall dissing of the church, abandonment of the traditional family structure and its relevance to the development of our nation and the people that run it and an abandonment of community, as evidenced by the many crime fighting programs we have today which involve restoring the community spirit. The degradation that has followed cannot be denied as we watch our politics and read about the violence and corruption in our streets and our culture and the loss of any value we had for our country and what it used to stand for. That's why we get comments like "God Damn America" and "to Hell with America" from today's liberalist leaders. That's why desecrating the American flag is of no consequence to today's leaders/judges. They no longer place any value on their homeland and therefore betray it with a clear concience. This must turn around or we will lose our nation and the sacrifices our founders built our heritage on. For some people, hatred and animosity is all they have to cling too in their lives and they want nothing less than to see all others just as miserable as they are. If we are going to change whats wrong in this country then we need to start looking in the mirror and pass judgment on ourselves and what our personal influence is having on other people in our lives. How often do we take for granted the emulations of others as truthful and in context when in truth, they were just parroting somebody else's bandwagon or gossip. It is more important than ever before that we take everything we hear or see with a grain of salt until we thoroughly research the information or assertions for ourselves and to the extreme so that we get the whole story and not just what was selected for us to see or hear so that we can make educated choices with the least harm to ourselves or others. We also need to use some common sense when we choose to do whatever we do through government with everybody else's money. Remember the addage, "Charity begins at home!" We need to take care of our own first and make sure our country is in the black, not the red. If we sink our boat, how can we rescue anybody else? We all end up drowning! Got to change our priorities! Got to examine our perspectives!

Well, that's my perspective as a commoner. I know what it's like to live out of the back of my car or seek shelter in an abandoned building. I know what it's like to have been subjected to abuse and on the recieving end of bullying and a dysfunctional family and what it's like to be called stupid and lazy because you can't keep up with other students. I've worked in dozens of trades from cowboying to ironwork, carpentry, heavy equipment operator/driver, missionary and a bunch of other things, all of which I used to supplement my education, some of which was formal and some of which was informal. I've lobby'd politicians, run for elected positions, been a single parent, widowed three times and had some of my children die from disease and drugs. These life experiences and working with others is where i've drawn my perspectives from and so what I have written about is coming from experience, not some professor's text book of theories and experiments. It's all down to earth and from this commoner's life at the bottom of the socioeconomic pyramid where all the other commoners eck out their living and their life. Take it for what its worth! I don't claim to be perfect or some kind of societal prodigy. I'm just a Commoner writing about what I have seen and heard and sharing it with others.

Lord Commonwealth.

www.ingramcontent.com/pod-product-compliance
Lightning Source LLC
Chambersburg PA
CBHW020655220526
45464CB00001B/443